DETAIL Practice

Concrete

Design
Construction
Examples

Martin Peck (Ed.)

Birkhäuser
Edition Detail

Authors:
Hubertus Adam
architecture critic, editor of *archithese*, Zürich
Andreas Bittis, Dipl.-Ing.
LiTraCon GmbH, Aachen/Csongrád
Susanne Frank, Dipl.-Ing. Architect
meck architekten, Munich
Andreas Hild, Dipl.-Ing. Architect
Hild & K Architekten, Munich
Roland Krippner, Dr.-Ing. Architect
assistant at the Chair of Building Technology,
Munich Technical University
Peter Lieblang, Dr.-Ing.
Bundesverband der Deutschen Zement-
industrie e.V., Berlin
Andreas Meck, Prof. Dipl.-Ing. Architect
meck architekten, Munich
Dionys Ottl, Dipl.-Ing. Architect
Hild & K Architekten, Munich
Martin Peck, Dipl.-Ing.,
Beton Marketing Süd GmbH, Munich
Christian Schätzke, Dipl.-Ing. Architect
scientific assistant at the Chair of Construction
II and Design, RWTH Aachen
Hartwig N. Schneider, Prof. Dipl.-Ing. Architect,
professor at the Chair of Construction II and
Design, RWTH Aachen

The publishers would like to thank Beton
Marketing Süd GmbH for their technical
advice and support.

Project manager:
Andrea Wiegelmann, Dipl.-Ing.

Editors:
Nicola Kollmann, Dipl.-Ing. (FH); Julia Liese,
Dipl.-Ing.; Sabine Schmid, Dipl.-Ing.
Drawings:
Nicola Kollmann, Dipl.-Ing. (FH); Andrea Saiko,
Dipl.-Ing. (FH)
German-English translation:
Gerd H. Söffker, Philip Thrift, Hannover

© 2006 Institut für internationale Architektur-
Dokumentation GmbH & Co. KG, Munich
An Edition DETAIL book

ISBN-10: 3-7643-7631-7
ISBN-13: 978-3-7643-7631-4

Printed on acid-free paper made from cellulose
bleached without the use of chlorine.

Typesetting & production:
Peter Gensmantel, Andrea Linke,
Roswitha Siegler, Simone Soesters

Printed by:
Wesel-Kommunikation
Baden-Baden

This book is also available in a German
language edition (ISBN 3-920034-13-9).

A CIP catalogue record for this book is available from the Library of Congress,
Washington D.C., USA.

Bibliographic information published by
Die Deutsche Bibliothek
Die Deutsche Bibliothek lists this publication in
the Deutsche Nationalbibliographie; detailed
bibliographic data is available on the internet
at http://dnb.ddb.de.

Institut für internationale
Architektur-Dokumentation GmbH & Co. KG
Sonnenstrasse 17, 80331 Munich, Germany
Tel: +49 (0)89 381620-0
Fax: +49 (0)89 398670
Internet: www.detail.de

Distribution Partner:
Birkhäuser – Publishers for Architecture
PO Box 133, 4010 Basel, Switzerland
Tel.: +41 61 2050707
Fax: +41 61 2050792
e-mail: sales@birkhauser.ch
www.birkhauser.ch

DETAIL Practice
Concrete

Contents

Concrete

The evolution of reinforced concrete

Martin Peck

The origins of building with concrete extend as far back as ancient times and started with the discovery and development of a concrete-like mineral building material that set, or hardened, hydraulically. Even though the technology of building with hydraulic building materials was in those times very different from today's concrete technology, the chemical-physical setting reactions between the raw materials were essentially the same, likewise the motivation for their use. Besides the use of timber, loam and rubble stones, building with a plastic material that set in moulds to form a solid mono-lithic mass was already known to builders in ancient times as an extremely advantageous method of building.

No definite date can be placed on the invention or discovery of hydraulic building materials. According to current knowledge, the first hydraulic binders comprised a mixture of lime and pozzolana (natural volcanic silica dust). The knowledge that after mixing with water these materials hardened to form an artificial stone was obviously available to Roman builders because many examples of its use have been found. The material used by the Romans is well documented and

1   Opera house in Santa Cruz, Tenerife, 2003, architect: Santiago Calatrava
2   Pantheon in Rome, c. 118–28 AD
3   Wholesale market hall in Munich, 1911; architect: Richard Schachner

2

3

some examples can still be seen today. It was called *opus caementitium*, and its usage spread very quickly. It was durable, easy to produce and the materials were readily available. The history books tell of water pipes and aqueducts, foundations and walls for buildings, all types of hydraulic structures for seawater and freshwater, plus more demanding structures such as bridges and palaces.

One of the best-known concrete structures from ancient times is the Pantheon in Rome (fig. 2). The construction of the hemispherical dome with an internal diameter exceeding 43 m marks a climax in the progress of architecture and engineering. The Pantheon is a feat of structural engineering which was obviously designed and built with great creativity and experience in terms of the details of the construction, building operations and building materials. The dome is made from a lightweight concrete mix which was obviously designed to reduce the self-weight of the structure. It was the advanced knowledge of the use of concrete as a building material that encouraged the designers to plan this unique project and, indeed, to build it.

As Rome's dominance spread across Europe, so the Roman methods of building with concrete also reached other parts of the continent. Examples of building with *opus caementitium* can still be seen today in almost all the larger Roman settlements. The spread of this form of construction was limited only by the fact that suitable raw materials such as lime and hydraulically active earths were not available everywhere.

After this early period of building with hydraulic building materials, much of the knowledge appears to have been lost in subsequent centuries. The dawn of a new age of building with concrete did not appear until the development of the first

cements in the 18th century. As the use of iron and steel for building were already spreading at this time, it was only a small step to combining steel with its good tensile properties and the lighter concrete with its good compressive qualities.

The invention of the composite building material reinforced concrete is attributed to the French gardener Joseph Monier (1823–1906). Monier tried to use thin-walled trough and slab-like concrete components, but these often developed cracks in use or broke completely. Only by placing iron wires in the wet concrete was Monier able to achieve components with sufficient stability. However, the obviousness of the composite effect of steel and concrete lets us suppose that reinforced concrete construction was not the work of just one person.

By the end of the 19th century it had become possible to describe mathematically the forces and stresses of even large and complex structures, i.e. to design and verify these by calculation, and this led to rapid developments in building with reinforced concrete. Whereas stone and timber, hitherto very popular materials, were more suitable for great architectural monuments, and steel as a building material was associated with high costs and high self-weight, the composite material reinforced concrete gave architects and structural engineers new design freedoms. This led to the intensive use of reinforced concrete in all categories of building. Huge structures were erected in short construction periods that had been impossible in the past, while techniques and quality underwent continuous improvement (fig. 3). The diversity and constructional opportunities of this method of construction inspired architects and engineers. By the start of the 20th century, building with concrete and reinforced concrete had become a permanent element in the building industry worldwide.

After the end of the Second World War the technical knowledge about reinforced concrete construction became globalised through an international transfer of expertise. Concrete in architecture and engineering, likewise the development of concrete technology, was taught at many international universities and became the subject of scientific research and development. This led to national standards for methods of building and building materials which supported the architect's freedom when using concrete and reinforced concrete. As a result, methods of construction employing concrete and reinforced concrete expanded rapidly. However, the concrete structures of the 1960s and 1970s, particularly in Europe, revealed severe shortcomings in design and construction that called for a fundamental rethink of the codes of practice to match the experiences of research and practice.

In the first half of the 20th century, architects used the sculptural possibilities of building with concrete and reinforced concrete with great artistic skill. Besides its use as a structural material, the visible concrete surface became increasingly important within the overall architectural concept. Architects such as Le Corbusier, Ludwig Mies van der Rohe and Louis I. Kahn integrated the visible concrete surface into their architectural ideas. Fairface concrete surfaces have remained topical as an element of architectural design to this day. No building material is used for engineering and architectural options to the same extent as concrete. Owing to its simple production and general availability, concrete is the building material of the 20th and 21st centuries (fig. 1).

The basics of concrete technology

Martin Peck

The architect or the structural engineer generally regards concrete as the finished component, in other words the shaped and hardened permanent material. Nevertheless, it is helpful to know about and to understand the composition of this building material and the building operations involved in its use.

Concrete was originally a three-part mixture of water, cement (the binder) and aggregate. The latter is usually a natural hard rock whose strength lies well above that of customary types of concrete. And the durability of the aggregate is usually virtually unlimited with respect to the possible corrosive influences to which a concrete component may be exposed. Strength and durability are the two most important properties of concrete and are controlled primarily through the cement and water contents in the mix. The properties of the cement and its composition are critical in this respect. But the findings of fundamental research and numerous developments have turned the three-part mixture into a five or multi-part composition. The original three components cement, water and aggregate have been joined by admixtures and additives.

Cement

Cement is produced by firing and subsequently grinding natural mineral raw materials obtained from quarries (fig. 4). These are earths and rocks which, owing to their geological composition, are suitable for producing cement and are found in almost all parts of the world in different national and regional concentrations. Firing at approx. 1400°C in a kiln produces so-called Portland cement clinker, which after grinding and adding calcium sulphate (gypsum) to control the hardening process becomes Portland cement. Pure Portland cement (European designation CEM I) is still widely used. However, from technical and ecological viewpoints it is no longer up to date. This is because the internationally agreed targets for reductions in carbon dioxide emissions in cement production and the improvement and control of the technical properties of a cement can only be achieved by adding further mineral components. Cement production therefore makes use of granulated blast-furnace slag, limestone dust, pulverised fuel ash (PFA), burnt shale or other suitable substances. These so-called additives and the quantities thereof are in most cases covered by standards. The use of additives results in cements with other standard designations, depending on the nature and quantity of the additive used, and the designation of a cement allows us to deduce its composition and some of its technical properties. Fig. 5 shows some main types of cement with their European standard designations and compositions.

Cements are classified according to the type of cement but are also divided into strength classes. The strength class of a cement is the critical variable for designing the strength of a type of concrete. The strength of a cement is primarily controlled via the degree of grinding of the

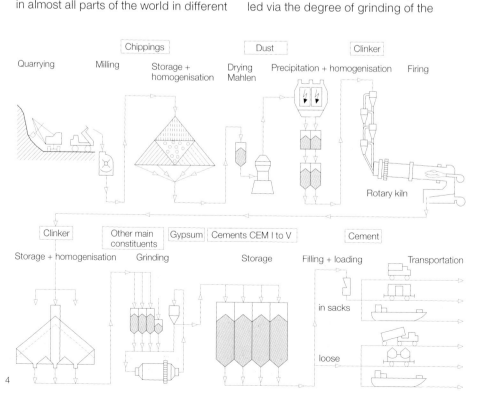

4 The manufacture of cement (dry method)

4

Cements and their composition

Main cement types	Name	Notation	Portland cement clinker — K	Granul. blast-furnace slag — S	Silica fume — D	Pozzolana natural — P	Pozzolana natural calcined — Q	Fly ash siliceous — V	Fly ash calcareous — W	Burnt shale — T	Limestone — L	Limestone — LL	Secondary constituents[1,2]
CEM I	Portland cement	CEM I	95–100	–	–	–	–	–	–	–	–	–	0–5
CEM II	Portland blast furnace cement	CEM II/A–S	80–94	6–20	–	–	–	–	–	–	–	–	0–5
		CEM II/B–S	65–79	21–35	–	–	–	–	–	–	–	–	0–5
	Portland silica fume cement	CEM II/A–D	90–94	–	6–10	–	–	–	–	–	–	–	0–5
	Portland pozzolana cement	CEM II/A–P	80–94	–	–	6–20	–	–	–	–	–	–	0–5
		CEM II/B–P	65–79	–	–	21–35	–	–	–	–	–	–	0–5
		CEM II/A–Q	80–94	–	–	–	6–20	–	–	–	–	–	0–5
		CEM II/B–Q	65–79	–	–	–	21–35	–	–	–	–	–	0–5
	Portland fly ash cement	CEM II/A–V	80–94	–	–	–	–	6–20	–	–	–	–	0–5
		CEM II/B–V	65–79	–	–	–	–	21–35	–	–	–	–	0–5
		CEM II/A–W	80–94	–	–	–	–	–	6–20	–	–	–	0–5
		CEM II/B–W	65–79	–	–	–	–	–	21–35	–	–	–	0–5
	Portland-burnt shale cement	CEM II/A–T	80–94	–	–	–	–	–	–	6–20	–	–	0–5
		CEM II/B–T	65–79	–	–	–	–	–	–	21–35	–	–	0–5
	Portland-limestone cement	CEM II/A–L	80–94	–	–	–	–	–	–	–	6–20	–	0–5
		CEM II/B–L	65–79	–	–	–	–	–	–	–	21–35	–	0–5
		CEM II/A–LL	80–94	–	–	–	–	–	–	–	–	6–20	0–5
		CEM II/B–LL	65–79	–	–	–	–	–	–	–	–	21–35	0–5
	Portland composite cement[3]	CEM II/A–M	80–94	←——————————— 6–20 ———————————→										0–5
		CEM II/B–M	65–79	←——————————— 21–35 ———————————→										0–5
CEM III	Blast-furnace cement	CEM III/A	35–64	36–65	–	–	–	–	–	–	–	–	0–5
		CEM III/B	20–34	66–80	–	–	–	–	–	–	–	–	0–5
		CEM III/C	5–19	81–95	–	–	–	–	–	–	–	–	0–5
CEM IV	Pozzolanic zement[3]	CEM IV/A	65–89	–	←————— 11–35 —————→				–	–	–	–	0–5
		CEM IV/B	45–64	–	←————— 36–55 —————→				–	–	–	–	0–5
CEM V	Composite cement	CEM V/A	40–64	18–30	–	←— 18–30 —→		–	–	–	–	–	0–5
		CEM V/B	20–38	31–50	–	←— 31–50 —→		–	–	–	–	–	0–5

[1] The values in the table relate to the total of the primary and secondary constituents (excluding calcium sulphate and cement additives).

[2] Substances added to cement as secondary constituents should not also be present in the cement as main constituents.

[3] The silica fume content is limited to 10%.

5

6   Natural rounded aggregates of different grades
    a   variegated gravel
    b, c rounded quartz
    d   quartz chippings

6a
b

cement. All properties that determine the mixing, placing and final properties of the hardened concrete should be designed into the cement. The technical properties of the various cements are covered by the respective materials standards and verified by the manufacturers through quality control procedures during production.

Water
Mixing cement with water produces so-called cement paste. A mixing ratio of about two parts by weight of cement to one part by weight of water is a technically favourable ratio that produces a slurry-like cement paste which sets to form so-called hydrated cement within about two to four hours. In order that this reaction can take place unhindered and achieve the desired result, the mixing water should not contain any constituents that might disturb the setting process, e.g. humic acid, certain industrial waste waters, etc. Drinking water is usually used for producing concrete. However, natural freshwater may be used if the batching plant is located near a suitable source, but this requires regular testing of the water because the content of certain constituents in the mixing water must be limited for technological reasons. In many countries the properties of mixing water for concrete are regulated by standards. Generally speaking, natural freshwater is well suited for use as mixing water in concrete. Even the water used in ready-mixed concrete works for cleaning plant and vehicles can be collected and re-used as mixing water after appropriate treatment and testing.

Aggregate
The aggregates used in concrete are mostly natural products (figs 6a–d and 8), but man-made, lightweight aggregates (e.g. expanded clay, foamed glass, etc.)

are often used to produce lightweight concrete of low density. The use of natural aggregate results in normal-weight concretes with densities ranging from about 2300 to 2500 kg/m³. If lightweight aggregates are employed, the density of a lightweight concrete with a dense microstructure can be reduced to values as low as 1200 kg/m³. Lightweight concretes with a dense microstructure are treated like normal-weight concretes from structural and constructional viewpoints, but possess a better thermal resistance and also permit use of more slender components owing to their lower self-weight.

Recycled aggregates have been approved for use in concrete for a number of years. This usually involves prepared scrap concrete which can be used in concretes for low to moderate technical specifications (see "Sustainability and recycling", pp. 45–47). The majority of natural gravel deposits, deposited by rivers or prehistoric moraines, are well suited to the production of concrete. The raw materials are sorted with sieves into various grades and added separately during the production of the concrete to form the desired blend of coarse and fine grades. Broken hard rock is often used in regions without deposits of natural gravel. This involves crushing the rock in mills and subsequently grading it. Concretes made using this type of aggregate usually require natural sands and a slight increase in the binder content in order to achieve the necessary workability. Aggregates for use in concrete are mostly covered by national standards.

Concrete additives and admixtures
The extra constituents that may be introduced into concrete are divided into additives and admixtures depending on their purpose.

Additives
Additives (fig. 7) are powder-type inorganic substances which are added to the concrete in relatively large quantities and, in technical terms, should be classed as part of the binder or, in the hardened concrete, the cement matrix (hydrated cement plus fine aggregate). Owing to the significant quantities used, additives must be taken into account when designing the concrete mix. The properties and composition of most additives are standardised. EN 206-1 regulates the use of additives in concrete throughout the European Union. This standard distinguishes between two types of additive:

• Type I additives are those without hydraulic properties, i.e. do not contribute to the strength development of the binder. Such substances can have a positive influence on the properties of the wet and hardened concrete owing to their physical effect within the particle matrix. These additives include rock dusts and pigments.
• Type II additives are primarily pulverised fuel ashes (PFA). They have a latent hydraulic effect, i.e. they are incited to a setting reaction by the hydraulic reaction partners contained in the cement and hence contribute to the strength. Pulverised fuel ashes are produced in power stations from the incombustible components of natural coals. They occur in the form of a fine dust and therefore require no grinding. The primarily spherical form of the particles means that the addition of pulverised fuel ash improves the workability of the wet concrete. Pulverised fuel ash can be added to the concrete mix in quantities ranging from about 30 to 80 kg/m³; in this way it is possible to save about 15 to 40 kg of cement respectively per cubic metre of concrete. However, their benefits are limited

c   d   7

Concrete admixtures/additives

Pigments

Essentially inert rock dust not contributing to strength

Inorganic, pozzolanic substances such as a pulverised fuel ash, silica fume as powder or in aqueous
suspension

Trass, which exhibits a pozzolanic reaction

because when used in large quantities
they can reduce the durability of the
concrete. This is why there is a limit
placed on the quantity used.
· Another type II additive is silica fume, a
technical by-product of silicon smelting.
This substance is considerably finer
than cement and is therefore suitable
for filling and packing the interstices
between particles in the wet and hardened concrete. The addition of silica
fume promotes and improves the bond
between the aggregate and the cement
matrix, which results in a substantial
improvement in the compressive
strength of the concrete. Silica fume
has rendered possible the production
of so-called high-strength concretes
(HSC) with compressive strengths
exceeding 60 N/mm². High-strength
concretes generally require special
planning measures because their mixing, placing and use requires special
knowledge and extra supervision.

Admixtures
Admixtures are highly effective chemical
substances, usually in liquid form, which
are added to the concrete during mixing
(fig. 11). The quantities used are relatively
small and are usually ignored when

designing the concrete mix. Admixtures
are used primarily to improve the properties of the wet concrete, i.e. to assist mixing and placing, and should not have any
negative effects on the hardened concrete. The values of the hardened concrete as required by the design must still
be reliably achieved even if admixtures
are employed.

The main application for admixtures is as
plasticisers or superplasticisers, for im-
proving the flowing properties of the wet
concrete. In order to guarantee the technical properties of the hardened concrete,
the amount of water used for mixing
should not exceed a defined maximum
value. Without the use of such plasticisers, the resulting concrete would be very
stiff, with only an earth-damp consistency,
and could not be placed in the formwork
using the customary methods. However,
the efficiency of the latest admixtures
enables the production of concretes with
very low water content but an easily work-
able, even fluid, consistence.
Retarders are less common but are useful
for controlling the solidification of the concrete in large-volume concrete components and for guaranteeing a wet joint
between individual lifts or pours. Stabilisers

can be used to assist the properties of
the wet concrete in mixes that may tend
to segregate owing to their composition.

Air entrainers are admixtures that are not
added to improve the properties of the
wet concrete, but instead to improve the
frost resistance of the hardened concrete.
Their effect on the properties of the wet
concrete is negligible. Air entrainers create spherical, microscopic air pores in the
structure of the hardened concrete. With
an appropriate size and distribution, they
act as expansion spaces when moisture
present in the system of pores within the
concrete freezes in cold weather. Current
standards prescribe the use of air entrainers in concrete components that may be
exposed to simultaneous saturation and
freezing in conjunction with de-icing salts.

**Division of responsibilities – properties
and composition of concrete**
The respective national standards prescribe indirectly the respective responsibilities of all participants with respect to
the design and construction of a concrete
structure. The structural engineer and the
contractor understand the concrete
purely by way of its technical properties.
The compressive strength class and the
durability requirements (exposure
classes, see "The properties of concrete",
p. 20) of the concrete are specified during the course of the structural design
work. Throughout the European Union,
the standardisation and specification of
the properties of the hardened concrete
deemed as required during the structural
design work are based on the system of
so-called exposure classes. The schedule of work drawn up by the building contractor results in requirements deemed
necessary for the wet concrete properties, such as consistency during placing
and the maximum size of aggregate.
These properties are ordered from the

Concrete aggregates to German standards

	Oven-dry density [t/m³]	Examples of aggregate
Lightweight aggregates	to DIN EN 13055 ≤ 2.0	Natural pumice, foamed slag, expanded clay, expanded shale
Normal-weight aggregates	to DIN EN 12620 > 2.0	Natural crushed or uncrushed dense rock (e.g. sand, gravel, chip pings), man-made crushed or un-crushed dense aggregates (e.g. blast-furnace slag in powder or lump form)
Heavy aggregates	technically > 3.0	Iron ore, baryte, steel shot

8

concrete supplier, often a ready-mixed concrete works, and must be verified by the supplier.

The design and calculation of a concrete mix and the technical proof of suitability of a concrete type are the responsibility of the concrete supplier. The supplier selects and varies the raw materials and the concrete mix within the limits specified by the standards in order to achieve the desired properties for the wet and hardened concrete, i.e. the supplier decides on the type and quantity of cement, water, aggregates, additives and admixtures. The architect and the structural engineer influence the concrete mix only in certain special cases; for example, the choice of cement or aggregate is of interest to the architect only if he or she has specified a particular appearance for the finished concrete surface. Even if further working of the concrete surface is necessary (sand-blasting, bush-hammering, etc.), the appearance of the finished surface will be affected to a certain extent by the choice of aggregate.

The production of concrete directly on the building site, with the contractor assuming responsibility for the mix and properties, requires more advanced expertise in concrete technology plus comprehensive facilities. This approach is primarily used when adequate supplies of ready-mixed concrete with the correct composition cannot be guaranteed (e.g. concrete roads, major projects).

Reinforcement

Concrete components are built with or without steel reinforcement (reinforced or plain concrete respectively) depending on the loads and form of construction. Like all building materials whose properties and behaviour are critical for the structural stability of a structure, the properties of the steel reinforcement and its use are covered in the respective national standards. Reinforcement is necessary when a concrete component is subjected to tension forces. Concrete is a mineral, brittle–elastic material capable of achieving high compressive strengths. However, its tensile strength – equal to about 10% of the compressive strength, even in high-strength concretes – is comparatively low. As the sudden, unannounced fracture behaviour of mineral building materials subjected to tensile stresses can lead to spontaneous failure of a component, the tensile strength of the concrete is usually ignored in the structural analysis, i.e. is taken to be zero. The tension forces occurring in a concrete component are therefore accommodated by incorporating steel reinforcement. In the structural analysis, the structural engineer calculates the parameters necessary for the reinforcement:

- the required total cross-sectional area of steel to accommodate the anticipated tension forces,
- the division of this total cross-sectional area of steel over sensible and technically beneficial bar diameters and bar pitches,
- the exact positions and arrangements of the reinforcing bars within the component, which is especially important because the reinforcement should be placed exactly in those parts of the component in which the largest tension forces occur.

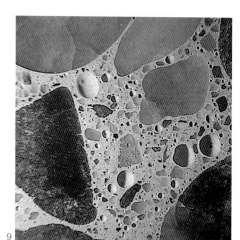

9

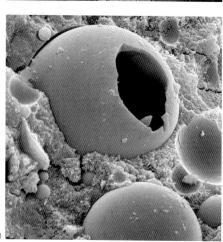

10

9   Visible micro air pores for increasing the frost resistance in a ground concrete surface
10 Embedded fly ash particle as revealed by the scanning electron microscope
12 Different types of steel reinforcement
13 Comparison of concrete mixes (parts by vol./m³)

Concrete additives/admixtures

Type	Abbreviation	Colour code [1]
Plasticiser	BV	yellow
Superplasticiser	FM	grey
Air entrainer	LP	blue
Waterproofer	DM	brown
Retarder	VZ	red
Accelerator	BE	green
Grouting aid	EH	white
Stabiliser	ST	violet
Chromate reducer	CR	pink
Recycling aid	RH	black

11 [1] The colour codes for containers were introduced to rule out mistakes.

The design and construction of concrete components is covered by the respective national standards. These codes of practice and methods of analysis are always based on a system of safety factors which regulates the production and supervision of concrete and its placing on site as well as the design of the components. For example, safety tolerances for steel and concrete are built into the structural analyses. These rule out later restrictions on use, damage to the building fabric or even the failure of a component due to a design based on inadequate reserves of strength.
In addition, there are general reinforcement codes for reinforced concrete components that must always be observed when manufacturing and placing the reinforcement. These include:

• Minimum diameter of bends:
Steel reinforcing bars are frequently used in a bent form. The bending is normally carried out on a machine by pressing the steel bar against a roller. A roller with an adequate diameter ensures that the reinforcing bar does not buckle at the point of bending and does not suffer internal fractures, cracking or embrittlement.
• Lap lengths between bars:
In the tension zone of a concrete component, laps in reinforcing bars should be avoided wherever possible in order to guarantee the reliable transfer of forces. However, if a lap is necessary, then the bars must overlap by a prescribed length so that the forces can be reliably transferred from one bar to the other.
• Anchorage lengths:
In order that a reinforcing bar can accommodate the tension forces it is designed to carry, both ends must be properly anchored in the concrete. The ends of the bars should be anchored in those parts of the concrete component with low loads.
• Concrete cover:
This is the depth of the concrete between the outer layer reinforcement and the surface of the component.

Sizing the concrete cover and ensuring it is maintained is especially important for the safety, reliability and durability of a reinforced concrete component. The concrete cover should not be so deep that it represents an unreinforced zone in which tension forces could lead directly to cracking or spalling. On the other hand, an adequately deep concrete cover is necessary to ensure a secure anchorage of the outer reinforcing bars and to protect them against corrosion.

Reinforced concrete is a composite system that functions in the long-term because concrete and steel have similar coefficients of thermal expansion and deform similarly over the normal range of temperatures and, as concrete and steel do not react chemically with each other, detrimental corrosion is also ruled out. Due to the lime content, the concrete matrix exhibits a strongly alkaline reaction in both the wet and hardened states. This 12 alkaline environment passivates the steel and protects it against corrosion. The passivation is highly effective and therefore even badly corroded reinforcing bars can be incorporated in the concrete. Although the concrete provides very effective, long-lasting corrosion protection for the steel, this system has its technical limits. For example, over longer periods of time, the natural carbon dioxide content of the air, together with the moisture in the air, tends to neutralise the alkaline content in the concrete. This reaction is known as carbonation and begins immediately after removing the formwork from the surface of any concrete component. The so-called carbonation front, i.e. the boundary between the already neutralised and the still alkaline concrete matrix, advances into the concrete component with the passage of time, although the process slows down progressively. Once the carbonation reaches the steel reinforcement, rusting may begin. The increase in volume associated with the formation of rust causes the concrete cover to break away, thus promoting further corrosion and leading to the characteristic corrosion damage. The time taken for the carbonation to penetrate as far as the reinforcement depends on the density and the depth of the concrete cover and the ambient conditions. External components in regions with a high humidity are particularly at risk because the alternating moisture conditions promote rapid carbonation and the corrosion of the depassivated reinforcement. By contrast, internal components do not usually exhibit corrosion damage even if the carbonation has reached the steel.
The concrete itself is not directly damaged by this process. In fact, the conversion of the unbonded lime in the concrete by the carbon dioxide from the air usually results in a marginal increase in strength. In the European system of exposure classes (see p. 20), carbonation is taken 13

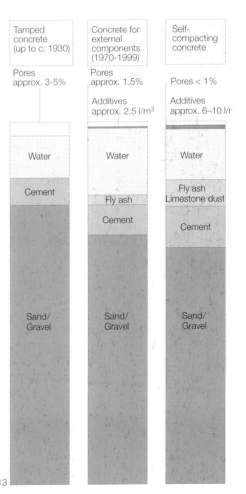

into account in classes XC1 to XC4. The design and careful construction of a reinforced concrete component according to the criteria of the appropriate exposure class should lead to the reinforcement being protected against corrosion by carbonation for at least 50 years.

Another major corrosion problem is that caused by chlorides, which are present in de-icing salts in high concentrations. However, they can also originate from chemical processes or natural waters (seawater, brine baths). Iron and chloride exhibit a very strong chemical affinity. Chloride corrosion can be far more aggressive and far more damaging for a component than carbonation. Chlorides can also cause corrosion of the reinforcement even if the surrounding concrete is not carbonated. If the other conditions for corrosion (humidity, oxygen) are present, severe damage to the reinforcement can rapidly occur. A chloride attack in aggressive environments can only be prevented by an adequately dense, deep concrete cover. Protective coverings or coatings are usually necessary on components in chloride-laden environments where cracking cannot be ruled out. In the European system of exposure classes (see p. 20), chloride attacks are considered in exposure classes XD1 to XD3
(de-icing salts, brine baths) and XS1 to XS3 (seawater).

The design of the reinforcement in reinforced concrete components is the job of the structural engineer and in the case of buildings normally has to be approved by the building authority responsible. The types and quantities of the reinforcement required in the components as well as the exact positions of the individual bars and meshes is shown on the working drawings, which also include details of concrete cover, compressive strength class and other relevant properties of the concrete. The working drawings are produced either by the structural engineer or by the contractor based on the structural engineer's design calculations.

General contractors almost always subcontract the bending and fixing (i.e. laying) of the reinforcement. In quality assurance terms (see "Quality and site management", pp. 68–71), it is not advisable to include clauses in the contract to prohibit such subcontracting work because some contractors do not have the facilities to produce the reinforcement themselves. The reinforcement is usually delivered to site cut to length and, if applicable, pre-

bent, bundled according to place of use, and then fixed in position.

After the reinforcement has been fixed, it should be checked by the structural engineer's site representative. If any of the following details are no longer accessible upon completion, they must be checked and approved beforehand:

- Check whether the type, quantity and positions of the reinforcement as installed comply with the working drawings.
- Check especially carefully that the prescribed concrete cover has been complied with. The concrete cover required depends on the exposure classes applicable, i.e. the ambient conditions, and can vary from face to face. The concrete cover is deemed to conform when no reinforcing bar is closer to the concrete surface than the nominal dimension c_{nom}, as given on the working drawings.
- Although rusty reinforcement may be used, the degree of corrosion should not be such that it leads to a reduction in the cross-section of the steel. In particular, check reinforcement that has been stored for a long time.
- When producing fair-face concrete surfaces, check that suitable bar spacers have been used on those surfaces. Such bar spacers for fair-face concrete are usually made from a cement-bonded material. Furthermore, make sure that all offcuts of tying wire and other debris are removed from the formwork prior to concreting.
- When reinforcing fair-face concrete floor slabs, it is impossible to prevent rust particles soiling the formwork during fixing of the reinforcement. The fine particles of rust drop down onto the formwork panels and stick to the release agent, and therefore cannot be completely removed with compressed air or water. The wet concrete pushes these particles ahead of itself as it flows into the formwork and tends to concentrate the soiling in certain areas. This leads to patches of brown discoloration on the soffit which are usually impossible to remove with subsequent cleaning. Such soiling can only be reliably avoided by using galvanised reinforcement. When fixing the reinforcement for a concrete slab, the operatives often work directly on the surface of the formwork, which frequently leads to damage and soiling on the inside face of the formwork caused by tools and safety shoes. Such imperfections in the form-

work can be seen later on the finished concrete soffit and can considerably spoil the quality of the surfaces. If a high-quality finish has been specified, operatives should therefore be instructed to change their shoes or cover them with felt shoe covers before walking on the inside face of the formwork. In addition, make sure that all offcuts of tying wire and other debris are removed from the formwork prior to concreting.
- When fixing reinforcement it often becomes very clear that it is not possible to maintain the intended bar pitches because the space within the formwork is too small. It takes experience to realise this simply by looking at the working drawings. In some cases the reinforcing bars in heavily loaded areas can be so close together that it is no longer possible to place the concrete properly. Sometimes it is sufficient to reduce the maximum aggregate size in order to ease placement. In addition, the vibrators necessary for compacting the concrete must be able to pass between the reinforcing bars. However, this is often impossible in heavily reinforced areas even though it is precisely at these points that intensive compaction is essential to ensure that the concrete surrounds the reinforcement fully without any voids. When designing the reinforcement, the structural engineer should always ensure that the concrete can be placed properly. Modifications to the reinforcement on site to ease placing of the concrete may only be carried out after consulting the structural engineer.

Formwork

The formwork is the mould in which the wet concrete hardens to become a concrete component. It must satisfy a few basic requirements:

- It must be possible to produce the formwork in the geometrical form given on the drawings and the formwork should not deform or distort significantly under the loads to be applied.
- The formwork must reliably accommodate the pressure of the wet concrete and, in some cases, the weight of the entire component (e.g. formwork to floor slabs). Additional loads and influences occur during concreting operations. The concrete compaction plant and the batch-type delivery of the wet concrete from crane skips can cause vibrations and impact loads on the formwork.

Further static and dynamic loads are caused by the concreting crew, construction plant and the pipes and hoses of concrete pumping plant.

· The formwork must be adequately sealed. The wet concrete should not lose any significant quantities of the fluid cement matrix through joints between parts of the formwork, or during compaction. However, a minor loss of liquid fine grout can never be completely excluded and therefore must be limited by careful construction of the formwork in order to avoid so-called bleeding and honeycombing. Such imperfections in fair-face concrete work are often impossible to make good satisfactorily and so lead to rejection and demolition of the component.

Besides these basic technical requirements, the formwork must satisfy economic criteria and ensure cost-effective concreting operations. In recent years, it has been primarily the development of formwork systems that has achieved noticeable cost-savings for concrete construction, and all the manufacturers of concrete formwork can now offer very effective systems. These consist of lightweight individual parts, also suitable for manual handling, which are set up and taken down with just a few operations and can carry large loads without distortion. Above all, the decrease in the self-weight of the individual system components has brought great advantages for site operations. Smaller cranes are adequate and they are even less in demand for formwork operations. Very tall structures with a more or less constant geometry can make use of climbing formwork or slipforms that require the help of cranes only in exceptional cases.
To optimise and limit the costs, formwork systems are frequently hired or leased. As the cost of dismantling, repairs and storage are included in the price, the total expenditure on formwork can be estimated more accurately.

The architect, as one member of the design team but also the project leader, is generally only involved in the selection and design of formwork when special requirements are placed on the appearance of the concrete surfaces. Generally, the choice and planning of the formwork is a task for the contractor alone.

Fair-face concrete surfaces
The production of fair-face concrete surfaces means that the designer, in placing particular requirements on the final appearance of the concrete surface, also places demands on the technical properties of the inside face of the formwork panels, i.e. in contact with the surface of the concrete. The characteristics of the inside face govern the appearance of the finished concrete. It is important to distinguish between the formwork and the formwork panels because the fair-face concrete specification inevitably affects the choice of formwork panels, but not necessarily the choice of formwork system. Only when a certain type of formwork panel is an intrinsic element in the design of a certain fair-face concrete surface should the designer specify it by name. Various national codes of practice and trade publications are available to help the designer plan fair-face concrete, also with regard to the choice and properties of formwork. In Germany the Deutscher Beton- und Bautechnikverein e.V. together with the Bundesverband der Deutschen Zementindustrie e.V. publish a data sheet on fair-face concrete which provides the design team with helpful advice on the following:

· Specifying the formwork panel class depending on a fair-face concrete class (see p. 98, fig. 5)
· Describing the criteria for the condition of individual formwork panel classes (see p. 101, fig. 9).
· Planning fair-face concrete, particularly with respect to formwork
· A comprehensive overview of customary formwork panels (see p. 101, fig. 9), together with a description of their technical features, the surface finishes to be expected and formwork re-use figures.
· Technical measures for achieving the required fair-face concrete class (see data sheet section 6 regarding workmanship requirements, and appendix); these measures should primarily help the contractor, but can also prove useful for the site supervision duties of the designer.

When planning fair-face concrete, architects and structural engineers should confine themselves to specifying the desired concrete surface or a number of basic technical properties of the formwork panel (e.g. timber, plastic, smooth, rough, textured, absorbent, non-absorbent, etc.). The choice of a suitable formwork panel and formwork system should be left to the contractor (and included in the contract provisions). The designers and contractor should use test surfaces to decide

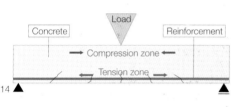

14

14 Reinforced concrete is a composite building material: the concrete withstands the compression forces, the steel reinforcement withstands the tension forces; in addition, the concrete protects the reinforcement against corrosion.
15 Placing wet concrete through an opening in the reinforcement in a heavily reinforced component

15

whether the formwork panel chosen by the contractor is suitable for producing the required surface finish. The choice of release agent should also play a role in tests with trial panels. Like the formwork panel itself, the release agent has an effect on the appearance of the final concrete surface and on the consistency of quality. The latest research findings concerning the interaction between formwork panel and concrete surface during the solidification and hardening of the concrete have revealed that the influence of the release agent (type, properties and thickness of coating) have a not inconsiderable effect on the appearance of the concrete surface. Like the formwork panels, the release agent should be chosen carefully based on the results of trials and not varied at random, perhaps simply according to price and availability.

When a high-quality fair-face concrete surface is intended, it is necessary to draw up a plan of the formwork. This should include the imprints of the formwork panel joints and the arrangement and nature of the formwork tie holes and plugs, which should be positioned to form a regular pattern. The use of simple patent wall formwork panels can usually be ruled out for high-quality fair-face concrete surfaces. Such formwork usually results in undesirable, small-format surface textures because the edges of the individual elements leave distinct imprints on the surface of the concrete. In addition, the element joints are often not sufficiently grout-tight. However, the large-format panels commonly used for fair-face concrete are available in fixed, maximum element sizes. Therefore, architects should base their ideas for the subdivision of the surface on a given product size because special sizes and high wastage through cutting can increase the cost of the formwork substantially.

In many cases it can be advantageous for the architect to specify the preparation of a formwork plan as part of the contractor's work. The drawings are then prepared in close cooperation between the architect and the contractor. This approach allows the architect to tap the contractor's knowledge of the market with respect to formwork and formwork systems. This cooperation often results in solutions that are satisfying in economic, technical and architectural terms. The preparation of the documentation by the contractor relieves the workload on the architect and ensures that the drawings are ready in time for construction.

Most manufacturers of formwork for concrete can provide extensive technical advice which is helpful to architects, engineers and contractors during all the design and construction phases. Many manufacturers publish technical brochures plus advice on site operations and design aspects, also in the form of software. Almost all suppliers of formwork for concrete will also design and build the formwork if requested, especially for demanding projects. An overview of the products and services on offer can be seen on the websites of the individual manufacturers and suppliers of formwork for concrete.

Standards and codes of practice

In most countries of the world, building with concrete is regulated by national standards or through the adaptation of external standards. A joint set of standards for building with concrete and reinforced concrete applies throughout the European Union. Although the vast majority of concrete applications are covered by the standards, there are some applications that fall outside the regulated framework. However, if the acknowledged codes of practice cannot be applied, this can lead to problems in approving the design and construction principles.

The principal standard for building with concrete in the European Union is European standard EN 206 part 1. This is a framework standard, the provisions of which must be fine-tuned by the building authorities of the member states to suit the respective national requirements of concrete construction based on climatic conditions, building traditions and the availability of raw materials. This is achieved by means of National Application Documents (NAD) – standardisation documents that usefully complement or restrict the provisions of EN 206 part 1. The EU member states are legally obliged to integrate the European and also the complementary national standards into their national building laws and statutory instruments. In doing so, the testing and approval principles for concrete structures in all member states are based on the same standard of safety. However, as the validity of the standards is restricted to loadbearing components, in individual cases it may be unclear – even to the building authorities responsible – whether a component or structure falls within the remit of the standard or not.

As the long-term safety of the loadbearing structure can only be guaranteed through a sufficiently durable construction, the EU regulations contain provisions regarding the durability of a concrete or reinforced concrete structure in addition to those for ultimate bearing capacity and serviceability. Durability is an economically motivated element because it deals with the protection and maintenance of the stock of buildings and structures, and therefore the new edition of the concrete standard in 2000 made durability a part of the design process. Based on knowledge about the corrosive influences and their effects on concrete or reinforced concrete components, the durability design factor integrated into this standard is intended to guarantee a minimum service life of 50 years. This tightening-up of the standard also makes this assumption realistic for severe conditions because even concrete structures designed and built to the preceding standards usually exhibit considerably longer lifespans.

The properties of concrete

Martin Peck

Design for durability is not a separate theoretical analysis. Instead, the structural engineer considers durability initially by determining the corrosive ambient conditions prevailing during the use of a building component. These are specified during the planning work by allocating components to a system of exposure classes (fig. 17). Depending on the appropriate exposure classes, the provisions of the standard specify a whole series of criteria for action that apply when designing the loadbearing structure, and during the production and placing of the concrete for the respective component. If these recommendations are adhered to during design and construction, the finished component has the potential to resist corrosive influences.

The system of exposure classes is based on a simple principle: the series of possible corrosive influences acting on a concrete or reinforced concrete component is essentially known. If we list the possible forms of corrosion according to their type and intensity, it is easy to deduce the exposure class system of the standards. Each exposure class represents a certain type of corrosive attack. As every type of corrosion can act on the component with varying intensity, the exposure class designations are supplemented by a number that corresponds to the intensity of the respective type of attack. The resulting system is ideal for designing concrete and reinforced concrete components realistically and economically to resist the anticipated corrosive influences caused by the ambient conditions. In order to help the structural engineer place the components in the right classes, the standard includes examples of components for each exposure class and each degree of attack, to act as a guide. There is also a whole series of publications available (see Appendix, pp. 108–109) that provide further help with the classification of customary building components. The table on the next page (fig. 17) shows the system of exposure classes together with the examples of building components allocated to them in the standard.

Basically, every concrete component covered by EN 206 part 1 must be allocated to its appropriate exposure class in the first phase of the planning because this is the only way to guarantee design, production and workmanship in accordance with the standard. This classification work is the task of the structural engineer, who is solely responsible for this aspect. The

responsibility of the structural engineer becomes clear during the ongoing planning work. As one of the aspects regulated by the exposure class appropriate to the component is the minimum compressive strength class, the structural analysis of a concrete component is hardly possible before the component has been allocated to the appropriate exposure class.

Compared to earlier provisions, the introduction of the exposure class system into European concrete standards has clarified and simplified the design for durability in the planning of concrete structures and components throughout the European Union. However, apart from a few exceptions, the exposure classes cover the design with respect to natural ambient conditions. The planning of building facilities in which the particular uses, processes or operations lead to corrosive conditions for the concrete components cannot always be dealt with solely by the corrosion cases in the standard. Such structures include those for chemical and electrochemical operations, dairies, warehouses for chemicals and biogas plants. The design of concrete components to withstand corrosive process conditions is always a special case. Such cases require the assistance of the client to determine the corrosive effects, plus appropriate experience and knowledge on the part of the design team, or the involvement of outside consultants.

In order to ensure that reinforced concrete structures possess adequate durability, both materials – concrete and steel – must exhibit appropriate resistance to the prevailing corrosive influences. The embedded steel reinforcement is protected against corrosion by the depth and quality of the protective concrete cover. This requires the steel reinforcement to be fully enclosed by the cement matrix. This condition is only possible in normal-weight, lightweight and heavy concretes with a dense microstructure. However, some lightweight concretes have a no-fines structure or a foam-like matrix that cannot be used as a loadbearing building material, at least not alone, but instead act as, for example, thermal insulation. Owing to their porous structure, such types of concrete cannot protect the steel reinforcement against ambient corrosive influences. These concretes are therefore not covered by the European standards for reinforced and prestressed concrete. Most of the concrete used in construction

Concrete as a building material

Types of attack and exposure classes

	Situation		Examples of components	Exposure class
No risk of attack or corrosion (components without reinforcement or embedded metal in ambient conditions not corrosive to concrete)				
	No attack		Components without reinforcement, in the soil without frost effects, chemical attack or abrasion; internal components without reinforcement	X0

Corrosion of reinforcement (only relevant for components with reinforcement or embedded metal)

through carbonation

Components with reinforcement or embedded metal which are exposed to the air and/or moisture	Dry or permanently wet		Components in interiors, also areas in housing with high humidity, components underwater	XC1
	Wet, seldom dry		Parts of water tanks/reservoirs, foundation components	XC2
	Moderate moisture		Components with frequent access for external air, open single-storey sheds, areas with high humidity used commercially or with access for the public, indoor swimming pools, cattle stalls	XC3
	Alternately wet and dry		External components directly exposed to rainfall	XC4

through chlorides (except in seawater)

Components with reinforcement or embedded metal which are exposed to water containing chloride	Moderate moisture		Components subjected to spray water from traffic areas, detached garages	XD1
	Wet, seldom dry		Components in brine baths, in industrial plants, and components exposed to chloride-laden process media	XD2
	Alternately wet and dry		Comp. subjected to splashing water from traffic areas, reinforced carriageways, parking decks	XD3

through chlorides in seawater

Components with reinforcement or embedded metal which are exposed to seawater or salt-laden air	Salt-laden air but no direct contact with seawater		External components in coastal regions	XS1
	Under seawater		Components permanently underwater	XS2
	Within tidal range, subjected to splashing and spray water		Quay walls	XS3

Corrosion of concrete (relevant for all plain concrete and reinforced concrete components)

through frost attack

Components exposed to considerable attack through freeze–thaw cycles	moderate water saturation	without de-icing	External components	XF1
		with de-icing	Components subjected to spray or splashing water from traffic pavements treated with de-icing salts, unless XF 4 applies	XF2
	severe water saturation	without de-icing	Open water tanks/reservoirs, components in the splash zone of freshwater	XF3
		with de-icing	Traffic pavements treated with de-icing salts, predominantly horizontal components subjected to splashing water from traffic pavements treated with de-icing salts, rotating scraper tracks in sewage treatment works, seawater components within the splash zone	XF4

through chemical attack

Components exposed to aggressive soils, groundwater, waste water or seawater according to DIN 1045-2 (table 2)	weak		Tanks in sewage treatment works, fertiliser silos	XA1
	moderate		Components in contact with seawater or aggressive soils	XA2
	severe		Cooling towers with exhaust-gas ducting, components in contact with chemically aggressive waste water, silage fodder silos and animal feeding tables	XA3

through abrasion

Surfaces of components exposed to considerable mechanical actions	moderate		Loadbearing or stabilising industrial floors subjected to the loads of pneumatically tyred vehicles	XM1
	severe		Loadbearing or stabilising industrial floors subjected to the loads of forklift trucks with pneumatic or solid rubber tyres	XM2
	very severe		Loadbearing or stabilising industrial floors subjected to the loads of forklift trucks with elastomeric or steel rollers, or tracked vehicles, hydraulic structures in rubble-laden waters (e.g. stilling basins)	XM3

17

is normal-weight concrete, i.e. concretes with a density of 2000–2600 kg/m³. Densities from 2350 to 2450 kg/m³ are common in Germany and Central Europe.

Wet concrete
Whereas the properties of the hardened concrete are specified at the planning stage, the requirements regarding the properties of the wet concrete primarily have to meet the needs of on-site operations. These requirements usually become known as the contractor plans his work, or immediately prior to ordering the concrete. The most important property of the wet concrete for site operations is the workability, now known as consistence, i.e. the flowing or deformation capacity. Requirements in this respect depend on the chosen method of transporting and placing the concrete, the geometry of the formwork and the amount of reinforcement in the component. The consistence for placing the concrete is therefore specified by the contractor. Only in exceptional cases, e.g. waterproof concrete, is it advisable to specify the consistence at the design stage. However, such instances still require good coordination between the design team and the contractor.

The contractor initially specifies the consistence of the concrete based on the chosen method of transporting the concrete. If the concrete is to be pumped, a suitable concrete mix and consistence must be selected. If large quantities of concrete are to be pumped in a short time, it is advisable to adjust the consistence of the concrete such that the maximum pumping capacity of the plant can be exploited. The method of compaction used when placing the concrete must also be coordinated with the concrete consistence. Complicated component and formwork geometries plus heavy reinforcement call for a more fluid consistence than large-volume slabs and similar components in which all zones are easily accessible for compaction.
As concrete cannot be produced exactly, its consistence can only be specified within consistence limits. This range of values can be classified by minimum and maximum measured values depending on the measuring techniques in use locally. In the territory covered by European standards, the concrete consistence is determined by the flow table test (Germany, Austria, Benelux and other countries) or the slump test (UK, Ireland). Both methods of measurement represent

simple tests which are easy to use on site and whose accuracy is usually adequate (figs 18–20). The test is carried out by placing a metal cone on a flat table (700 × 700 mm) and filling the cone with the concrete. The metal cone is then lifted off and the wet concrete spreads out on the table. In the flow table test, one side of the table is lifted and dropped 15 times. This results in a circular pad of wet concrete whose diameter is then measured at two points at right-angles to each other. The average value of the two measurements determines the consistence. This dimension for standard concretes ranges from 340 to 700 mm, which are assigned to consistence classes F1 to F6 in EN 206 part 1. The range of each class is 60 mm. If the standard classes are not adequate for a certain building task (e.g. fair-face concrete), a fixed target value can be specified with a tolerance of ±30 mm to define an individual class with the standard tolerance. If, for technical reasons, it is necessary to restrict the tolerance of the class even further, then this is possible, but will generally mean an increase in price owing to the greater care required during production. Tolerances < 40 mm (±20 mm) cannot be reliably produced with conventional plant and, owing to the scatter of test results, are hardly measurable. Fig. 20 shows the consistence classes with their associated dimensions and descriptions.
Class F1 denotes a very stiff consistence with a flow diameter of max. 340 mm. The subsequent classes F2 to F5 each have a tolerance range of 60 mm. Class F6 denotes a very fluid consistence with a flow diameter of 630–700 mm. Classes F2 and F3 are generally used for buildings. The production of concretes with consistence classes F4 to F6 requires the use of an efficient plasticiser.

There is a close relationship between the effective water/cement (w/c) ratio (= ratio of water to cement by mass) and compressive strength and durability, i.e. the most important hardened concrete properties. Traditional concrete technology has therefore always tried to keep the water content in concrete as low as possible in order to minimise the comparatively expensive cement – for a constant w/c ratio. This was the reason for the earth-damp consistence of the majority of concrete produced and placed in the late 19th and early 20th centuries. This consistence is very difficult to transport and was mainly compacted by tamping manually (so-called tamped concrete). After

18

19

the Second World War the production, transport and placing of concrete was increasingly mechanised and automated. As the tamping method cannot be readily mechanised and compaction by tamping became less and less practicable as reinforcement densities increased, more plastic consistencies were called for. The cement content in concrete gradually climbed in order to achieve the necessary placing consistence while maintaining a constant water/cement ratio. Once plasticisers appeared in the 1970s, it became possible to produce ever softer concrete consistencies without increasing the water/cement ratio. Since then, the placing properties of wet concrete have been increasingly controlled by additives, the effectiveness of which has been improved further and further. Technology will soon make it possible to produce an almost fluid consistence with a comparatively low water content.

In the 1990s a further technological advancement in the form of the discovery of new types of highly efficient additives enabled the consistence necessary for site operations to be essentially divorced from the water content of the concrete. As it became possible to produce virtually any required consistence with very low water contents, the strength of the concrete and the freedom of choice for contractors regarding consistence could be guaranteed independently. Whereas in the past the on-site placement methods had to be geared to the technical possibilities for controlling the consistence, it is now possible to arrange concrete placement primarily according to economic criteria because almost any desired consistence can be ordered and supplied. Concrete suppliers are making use of modern additives technology and are increasingly offering types of concrete with very fluid consistencies. The devel-

opment of easily compacted concretes with consistence classes F5 and F6 mean that in many cases it is possible to exploit the maximum pumping capacity of modern concrete pumps and to reduce the amount of local compaction. Indeed, the use of these fluid consistencies has resulted in compaction proving unnecessary for large-volume and slab-like components such as foundations, ground slabs and floor slabs. In vertical components (columns and walls) such a procedure can result in severe "honeycombing" on the side forms, which reduces the concrete cover and can considerably impair the quality of fair-face concrete surfaces.

A special type of concrete closely associated with the aforementioned additives · technology is self-compacting concrete. The production of this type of concrete essentially exploits to the full the possibilities of current superplasticiser technology. Self-compacting concretes require absolutely no compaction, even in complex component geometries, and spread out, compact and deaerate in the formwork through the action of gravity alone. Self-compacting concrete contains a large proportion of very fluid binder paste, which is usually produced by adding a generous amount of type I or type II additive. The coarse aggregate is transported in this fluid matrix with its honey-like consistence. Although self-compacting concretes flow very easily, they have an extremely low water content. Prior to introducing the additive, they are merely earth-damp and can even be produced with water/cement ratios well below 0.40 – extremely unusual in the past. Owing to the high binder content and extremely low water content, self-compacting concretes can achieve impressive hardened concrete properties. The compressive strength values achieved in practice are often higher than those planned – a typical

20

Consistence classes

Class	Flow limits [mm]	Consistence
F1	≤ 340	stiff
F2	350 to 410	plastic
F3	420 to 480	soft
F4	490 to 550	very soft
F5	560 to 620	fluid
F6	≥ 630	very fluid

feature of self-compacting concrete. The rheological system of self-compacting concrete flows more readily than conventional concretes, but it exhibits considerable viscosity. Self-compacting concretes spread out and deaerate by themselves and flow even into the tightest of spaces in the formwork. But to do this they require considerably more time than a concrete with a soft consistence used in conjunction with compaction techniques. This honey-like flow behaviour in the transportation of the concrete ensures that the heavy aggregate particles do not sink through the fluid matrix and cause the mix to segregate. Self-compacting concrete has been used with great success in precasting works, but owing to the metering accuracy required, can only be supplied as ready-mixed concrete if supplementary testing and supervision measures are employed.

As the production of fair-face concrete usually calls for a somewhat higher binder and matrix content, the question is whether self-compacting concrete would be particularly suitable for this type of application. However, experience with the production of fair-face concrete using concretes with consistence classes F5 and F6 is mixed. This shows that the production of fair-face concrete is only partially dependent on the concrete mix and the consistence, and that the effects of workmanship, formwork panels, release agent and component geometry can be more important (see "Fair-face concrete – design and construction", pp. 90–91).

Hardened concrete

The setting characteristic of the cement also governs the solidification and hardening behaviour of the concrete. Provided a retarder has not been used, concrete usually begins to solidify after about 2–2.5 hours. This solidification is not a sudden process, but rather manifests itself after 1–1.5 hours as the wet concrete begins to stiffen noticeably. The solidification of the concrete signals the transition from the plastic state of the wet concrete to the brittle–elastic state of the hardened concrete. During this phase transition, the hydration of the cement, i.e. its reaction with the water in the concrete to form hydrated cement, takes place with maximum intensity. Most of the water present in the microstructure of the concrete is consumed and bonded into the hydrated cement and the remaining unbonded water is forced into the pore spaces created by the recrystallisation of the hydrated cement. As crystal growth progresses, so this consumes further water and the pore spaces become ever smaller. Once the individual cement particles merge with the growing crystals and are no longer free to move, the concrete solidifies and begins to harden. Hardening is defined as the development of strength in concrete that has already solidified. The course of the hardening process and hence the development of strength depends on a number of factors, including the type of cement and the water/cement ratio. At average temperatures, the types of concrete customarily used for building work develop 30–70% of their target strength during the time between placing the concrete and striking the formwork after about 1–3 days.

18 Measuring the consistence (i.e. workability) of normal-weight concrete: flow table test
19 Measuring the consistence of self-compacting concrete
21 In situ concrete component made from self-compacting concrete, PHAENO Science Centre, Wolfsburg, Germany, 2005; architect: Zaha Hadid, with Mayer/Bährle

22 a

b

The compressive strength is the most important technical property of hardened concrete. Concrete components are designed by the structural engineer with a so-called characteristic strength, i.e. a compressive strength assumed for the theoretical design model. This strength assumption is only valid if the concrete in the component achieves or exceeds the theoretical compressive strength with sufficient reliability. Every design system therefore incorporates a number of safety factors to compensate for possible tolerances resulting from the assumptions regarding the effective actions, the modelling of the structural system and deviations in the materials. Such deviations can ensue through inaccuracies in the concrete mix, or during the production or concreting operations on site. In order to guarantee that the actual deviations in the material do not exceed the safety factors used in the structural analysis, a subsequent system of safety factors solely for the planning and the verification of the concrete compressive strength is necessary. As sufficiently accurate verification of the compressive strength is only possible with a destructive test, there is no way of testing the compressive strength directly on the built component. Instead, the tests are carried out on test cubes that are made during the production and placing of the concrete for a concrete component. These are stored under standardised conditions, e.g. underwater at approx. 20 °C, and tested after 28 days (figs 22a and 22b). These test results are representative of the concrete in the entire component.

The standardised storage and testing conditions are necessary in order to achieve meaningful and unified compressive strength values. The climatic conditions of the standardised storage prior to testing are very favourable for the hardening process of the concrete. Testing the cubes for their compressive strength reveals the potential compressive strength, i.e. the compressive strength that the concrete has achieved after 28 days under these very favourable hardening conditions. But as the hardening conditions on the structure itself are not normally as favourable as the standardised conditions, the 28-day value measured in the laboratory is usually much higher than the strength in the component at the same time. In the case of especially unfavourable hardening conditions, e.g. in winter, the concrete in the structure itself can take much longer than 28 days to reach the compressive strength measured in the laboratory after 28 days. However, unfavourable hardening conditions, e.g. cold weather, can only slow down the strength development in the component, not stop it entirely in the long-term. As the concrete in the structure continues to develop its strength up to its technical limit, it will with all probability reach, in most cases even clearly exceed, the compressive strength measured in the laboratory after 28 days.

22 Testing the compressive strength
   a at start of loading
   b cube at failure

The effective safety margin between the compressive strength assumed in the structural analysis and the compressive strength as tested ensues from the permissible tolerances. The upper compressive strength values of the structural analysis, including all safety factors for loading assumptions, modelling and material deviations, at the same time form the lower statistical thresholds for the values established in practical compressive strength tests on concrete taken from the structure. This means that the probability of failure of a component due to inadequate concrete strength can be ruled out statistically (with adequate safety margins). A slow strength development of the concrete in the structure at a young age is only interesting from the on-site operations viewpoint. Such slow development may result in longer striking times, longer curing times or longer propping of slabs and beams, but does not mean that the concrete itself is of inferior quality.

The system of safety factors for assuming and verifying the compressive strength of the concrete is covered by building codes in all countries. A system of compressive strength classes in the respective standards for concrete building work enables clear technical communication between the design team, the concrete supplier (ready-mixed concrete works) and the contractor responsible for placing the concrete. In the standards of Central Europe the compressive strength class in the current standards is denoted by the code letter C (= concrete) and two figures (e.g. C 25/30). The designation by means of these two values is explained by the different geometries of the test samples used. In some countries the compressive strength test is carried out using cylindrical samples instead of cubes, which results in lower compressive strength values than those obtained using cubes made from exactly the same concrete. This is why the pair of figures was necessary when rewriting national codes for use at European level.

Compressive strength classes for normal-weight and heavy concrete

Compressive strength class	$f_{ck, cyl}$ [N/mm^2] [1]	$f_{ck, cube}$ [N/mm^2] [2]	Type of concrete
C 8/10	8	10	
C 12/15	12	15	
C 16/20	16	20	
C 20/25	20	25	
C 25/30	25	30	
C 30/37	30	37	normal-weight
C 35/45	35	45	
C 40/50	40	50	
C 45/55	45	55	
C 50/60	50	60	
C 55/67	55	67	
C 60/75	60	75	
C 70/85	70	85	
C 80/95	80	95	high-strength
C 90/105 [3]	90	105	
C 100/115 [3]	100	115	

[1] $f_{ck, cyl}$ = characteristic strength of cylinders, 150 mm dia. × 300 mm long, 28 days old, stored according to DIN EN 12390-2
[2] $f_{ck, cube}$ = characteristic strength of cubes, 150 × 150 × 150 mm, 28 days old, stored according to DIN EN 12390-2
23 [3] Requires general building authority approval or approval for individual project

Translucent concrete

Andreas Bittis

Until now, Superman was the only being that could see through walls! His special x-ray laser eyes possessed two interesting properties: firstly, he was in the position to turn any solid wall into a type of revealing x-ray screen, and secondly, he could use his laser eyes to burn through the hardest steels, or weld together the most diverse materials. Nearly 70 years after the first Superman comics appeared, the Fraunhofer Institute declared photonics to be one of the leading innovations of the 21st century. At the same time, architects and scientists drew attention to themselves with projects and prototypes that allowed solid walls to become permeable to light.

One of the first of these was the Japanese architect Toyo Ito, who developed his building facades as "permeable screens" to reflect the exterior inside and the interior outside. The aim here is not to break down the facade in the tradition of Mies van der Rohe, but rather to create a building envelope that constantly changes. This play between lightweight and heavyweight, bright and dark, depth and superficiality is especially successful on the recently opened Performing Arts Centre in the Japanese city of Matsumoto (figs 2

and 3). In this project the facade was designed as a self-supporting curtain wall made of precast concrete elements with translucent inclusions. Despite the solid impression, this is in reality a steel assembly clad with 25 mm concrete panels on both sides. Identical cut-outs in both surfaces were formed during assembly with specially made cylindrical polycarbonate elements. The result is a wall whose appearance allows visitors to this concert hall to forget that concrete is often regarded as a cold material. Instead, concert-goers seem to feel the need to get to grips with – in the truest sense of the word – this breakdown in materialness. Countless fingerprints bear witness to this! The concrete loses its coldness and "untouchability".

Another Japanese architect, Jun Aoki, uses concrete in a similarly playful way in his latest project. Having already used metal fabrics to create an unmistakable transparent feeling in the first Japanese flagship store for a French manufacturer of exclusive leather goods, he has managed to achieve a very special setting in his second project in Tokyo: a four-storey concrete cube, which during the day is conspicuous due to its fine detailing and random patterns, turns into an impressive

1 Store in Tokyo, 2004; architect: Jun Aoki
2, 3 Matsumoto Performing Arts Centre, 2004;
   architect: Toyo Ito

3

play of light during the hours of darkness. This is made possible by the pieces of marble cast into the concrete panels of the facade. During daylight hours they add texture to the facade; at night they unfold to form a three-dimensional Sierpinski Carpet[1] (fig. 1).

The astonishing thing about these and other, similar projects is that it is only now that they are being realised, that concrete is presenting itself as a composite material for mixing and experimenting with other materials. The Romans were using it long before modern concrete discovered

it as a projection screen for light and shade as well as a universally applicable building material. Concrete was not discovered again until the 19th century – and immediately reduced to the technological options in the sense of "higher, stronger, further". The German engineer Werner Sobek describes it thus: "Wherever concrete cannot be or may not be covered with another material, ... it always invites criticism, rejection, vandalism. The ... user buys the product ... not because of its aesthetic qualities, but rather because of the absence of alternatives. ... We must therefore ... once again begin

our search for the component forms, material surfaces and colours that are truly appropriate to this wonderful building material.
A century of advancement in the technical qualities should now be followed by years of advancement in the aesthetic qualities."
Numerous experiments and prototype developments in recent years have taken the first steps in this direction. However, all these new developments are still waiting for use on a wide scale, not least because many of the technical details are not yet available.

4

5

6

Development

Taking the well-known terrazzo flooring for his inspiration, Jerry Milton Tjon-Tam-Sin, working in the Netherlands, called his material – a mixture of cement and glass – Verrazzo (fig. 5). Thanks to the use of cement with a low effective alkaline content and carefully controlled cement properties, it has been possible to guarantee an extremely strong bond between the two raw materials. According to information provided by the manufacturer, Verrazzo can be used for structural purposes because the material achieves compressive strengths similar to high-strength concrete. Consequently, elements with a thickness of just 3 mm are feasible. Frost resistance and behaviour in fire are similar to that of normal-weight concrete. Verrazzo can be used as in situ concrete – with conventional steel reinforcement – and also in precast concrete elements. But to date there are no examples of its use.

Christian Meyer from New York's Columbia University is pursuing a similar path. In his attempts to replace the raw materials in concrete by recycled materials, he was able to substitute crushed recycled glass for the sand and gravel. In order to rule out any reaction between the glass and the alkaline constituents of the cement, a part of the cement was replaced by metakaolin, which lowers the alkaline content (fig. 6).

In the meantime, translucent floor tiles made from this recycled material are being manufactured and marketed.[2] The architect can choose between numerous sizes (12 × 12, 18 × 18, 24 × 24, 30 × 30 and 36 × 36 cm), different material thicknesses (20–27.5 mm) and 36 colours. In the course of further research, Meyer discovered that some types of sludge dredged up every day from the navigation channels of New York's harbour absorb the alkaline constituents far better

than the metakaolin he has been using so far. We eagerly await the next chapter in this "eco-concrete" story!

An Indian based in Detroit, Abhinand Lath, has developed a tile[3] which contains glass fibres that react autonomously to changing light intensities or shadows – without the need for any light source behind them. Two different types of tile are currently available: a cement-bonded variation (Terrazzo) and one based on an acrylic polymer (Scintilla). Both are available in different thicknesses (1/2 and 1 in) and dimensions (4 × 4, 8 × 4, 6 × 6, 12 × 6 and 12 × 12 in). The first projects – from furniture to floor mosaics – have already been realised.

Translucent concrete

Will Wittig from the University of Detroit Mercy was interested in the question of whether concrete as a solid building material can also be used in a translucent form such as alabaster or Carrara marble – but without the high cost. Guided by this idea, he mixed white silicate, white Portland cement and short glass fibres to form a paste-like mixture. The result was extremely thin (as little as 1 mm) concrete tiles which although light-permeable could withstand neither rain nor wind. So Wittig began searching for a suitable backing material, which turned out to be everyday polycarbonate sheeting. He has prepared and researched a number of prototypes, but none has yet been used for any practical applications.

In 2001 an American, Bill Price, announced that he had developed a form of "translucent concrete". At that time he had just left the OMA architectural practice and was looking for manufacturers with whom he could put his idea into practice. This had been preceded by research and tests for the concert hall in Porto. During

4 Paving flags made from light-permeable concrete, Stureplan, Stockholm, 2002 (competition entry); architects: E. Giovannione, G. Hildén, Á. Losonczi, A. Lucca
5 Verrazzo floor covering; material development: Jerry Milton Tjon-Tam-Sin
6 Terra Paving floor tiles, recycled glass aggregate; material development: Christian Meyer

the trials he had replaced conventional aggregates by fragments of plastic or glass, had used organic, light-permeable binders instead of cement, and had substituted translucent polycarbonate rods for the conventional steel reinforcement. This proved to be a very time-consuming business because all the parameters had to be coordinated with each other. And this explains why Price has not yet revealed any of the technical data relating to his material. His Pixel Chapel – a small building, not yet realised, in which the beauty of translucent walls can be surmised from models and computer simulations – is intended to be built from 1.5 × 5 m prefabricated panels 100 mm thick, the so-called Pixel Panels. The light permeability is achieved through translucent polycarbonate rods of different sizes and lengths.

Another method for the production of translucent concrete was developed by the Hungarian architect Áron Losonczi.[4] LiTraCon© (= Light Transmitting Concrete) is a concrete material with light-directing properties (fig. 4). In this material, fibre optics – like those used in endoscopy or telecommunications – are cast into the concrete and therefore transmit light virtually without loss from one side of a concrete wall to the other (fig. 7). The concrete appears to be illuminated from within; shadows and silhouettes appear quite distinctly on the non-illuminated side (fig. 9). Tests have revealed that the light transmission will drop by just 10 % or so over 20 years. What this means for the fibres used is that at least 60 % of the incident light will still pass through the wall. The fibres transmit the light without significant loss of intensity over distances of up to 20 m. This opens up new options for supplying daylight or artificial light to subterranean spaces such as basement garages and underground stations; even colours are transmitted.

The proportion of fibre optics in the material is merely 5 % by vol. In technological terms this is therefore concrete with its customary technical properties, which have been confirmed in strength tests. Even compressive strength class C 50/60 has been achieved with suitable concrete mixes. The fibres, which can have any diameter between 2 µm and 2 mm as required, are fully enclosed by and fully structurally bonded within the concrete matrix. Owing to the fragility of the fibre optics, the elements are produced individually as precast concrete units and then delivered to the building site. Besides the size of the elements (fig. 8), the architect can determine the arrangement of the fibres (random, in a pattern, or in the form of a logo). The first projects have already been realised in Hungary. For example, a sunshading element measuring 400 × 800 mm was built for a private house near Budapest. The official monument marking Hungary's entry into the European Union, the "Eurogate", is much larger – a 4 m high triangular pillar with backlighting column and canopy (fig. 10).

Outlook

All the research, prototypes and products signal the start of developments that aim to make concrete "intelligent". For example, the Boston-based architectural practice of Kennedy & Violich uses sensor-controlled diodes in the concrete in order to illuminate footpaths in the dark. Their "Smart Concrete" is still undergoing development. The situation is similar for the so-called Smart Brick, developed by Chang Liu at the Center for Nanoscale Science & Technology, University of Illinois. Besides sensors and microelectronics, the brick contains a transmitter that measures the external temperature, vibra-

7

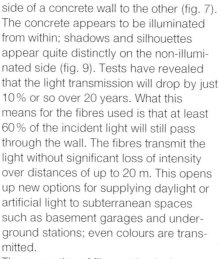

8

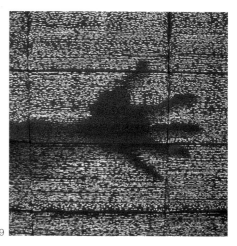

9

tions and settlement in and around the building, and sends this information to a facility management centre or an emergency system. Light-permeable concrete with its embedded fibre optics provides a useful complement to this system. If we consider the amount of data that is already being transmitted these days via fibre optic cables, e.g. broadband telecommunications, we can find many opportunities to use walls for multimedia applications. LEDs, USB ports and microsensors integrated into translucent concrete walls render it possible to transmit any information from outside to inside (e.g. humidity, temperature, wind speed), from inside to outside (e.g. advertising films, photographs, colours, textures), or within the building. The building material therefore takes on both aesthetic and functional tasks which enable designers of buildings to explore new paths and create interactive environments between light and concrete. The wall becomes simultaneously a screen and a scanner and overcomes the laws of heaviness and depth: concrete surface and projection medium merge into one.

10

[1] The Sierpinski Carpet is a fractal devised by the mathematician Waclaw Sierpinski. It begins with a square. The square is cut into nine congruent subsquares in a 3 x 3 grid, and the central sub-square is removed. The same procedure is then applied recursively to the remaining eight sub-squares, ad infinitum.
[2] Terra Paving; www.wausautile.com
[3] SensiTile™; www.sensitile.com
[4] LiTraCon©; www.litracon.com

7–9 LiTraCon© light-permeable concrete
10 Wall made from light-permeable concrete, "Eurogate", Komaróm, Hungary, 2004; design: Áron Losonczi

Concrete as a building material

Textile-reinforced concrete

Christian Schätzke
Hartwig N. Schneider

Properties and how it works

Textile-reinforced concrete represents one of the most remarkable contemporary developments in concrete technology and is not without its repercussions for the work of architects and engineers. Textile-reinforced concrete is a further development of fibre-reinforced concrete, but differs from this in that this new building material contains no short fibres. Instead it uses commercial textiles – weaves and nets – made from glass, carbon or aramid fibres as the reinforcing material, which enables the reinforcement to be incorporated exactly as required and hence much more economically.

A good bond between the textile reinforcement and the enclosing concrete matrix is essential to ensure that the material functions as intended. Very fluid, fine concrete mixes with a maximum particle size of 1 mm are therefore used for textile-reinforced concrete. The combination of these two components determines the main characteristics of the new building material. The use of textile reinforcement obviates the need for a deep concrete cover to protect the reinforcement against corrosion. This in turn leads to components with thin walls of just 10–20 mm. Furthermore, thanks to the self-compacting property of the fluid, fine concrete, it is possible to produce high-quality fair-face concrete surfaces and very accurate contours. Building performance characteristics also benefit from the dense microstructure of the fine concrete mix. Despite such thin components, it is possible to build waterproof elements and also achieve relatively good fire resistance figures. For example, the first fire tests have resulted in fire resistance class F30 when using alkali-resistant glass (AR glass) as the reinforcing material, and F60 for carbon. The thin components in particular and the associated saving in weight are among the most important properties of textile-reinforced concrete, and render possible lightweight forms of construction with reduced consumption of materials.

Such properties lead us to expect the widespread use of textile-reinforced concrete in all branches of architecture. From the loadbearing structure to the building envelope, fitting-out to internal finishes.

Materials

Concrete

The concrete mix employed as the matrix is different to that of normal-weight concrete. The most conspicuous difference is the small maximum particle size (approx. 1 mm). In addition, silica fume, fly ash or similar products can be used to improve the workability. When using AR glass, these constituents have a positive effect on the long-term properties. It should be noted that the small maximum particle size results in a higher binder requirement, which can lead to correspondingly higher shrinkage and creep deformations.[1]

Textile reinforcement

The raw materials for the textile reinforcement are high-performance technical fibres made from alkali-resistant glass, carbon, aramid or synthetic materials (polypropylene, PVA, etc.). When using glass, the corrosion of the glass by the alkaline environment in the concrete is a crucial factor with respect to the durability of the composite material. AR glass is therefore used, which when combined with low-alkali concrete mixes results in adequate durability. The raw materials are usually in the form of filaments with

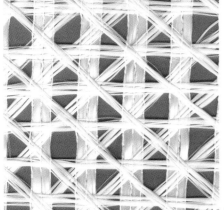

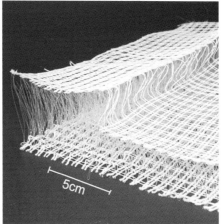

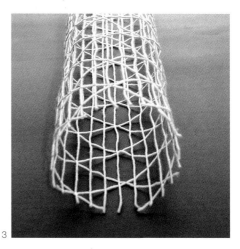

diameters of 10–30 µm. Hundreds or even thousands of these filaments are grouped together into bundles, the filament yarn, during manufacture. These yarns are then used to fabricate technical textiles such as nets, braids, weaves or meshes. The most common textile reinforcing materials are in the form of multiaxial nets, spacer fabrics and seamless textile tubes.

Multiaxial nets consist of several layers of fibre bundles (rovings) or yarns which are arranged in different directions (at angles of 0°, +45°, -45° or 90° – but essentially parallel to the plane of the textile) which are joined together by knitting threads (fig. 1).

Spacer fabrics are three-dimensional textiles in which two net layers are joined together by spacer threads perpendicular to the plane of the textile which hold the nets a certain distance apart. The spacing of the two net surfaces can vary (fig. 2). Spacer fabrics are used where it is important to achieve a defined distance between the layers of reinforcement, e.g. in planar components with several layers of reinforcement.

Seamless textile tubes are three-dimensional textiles with a closed, pipe-like cross-section. The individual rovings or yarns run parallel to the axis of the tube and at angles of 20–80° (fig. 3). Seamless textile tubes are primarily used for reinforcing hollow sections.

Manufacture

The manufacturing techniques used to date can be broken down into series (individual) production and continuous or semi-continuous production. Series production mainly makes use of casting, injecting and laminating. Continuous production is divided into the Sheetcrete and Wellcrete methods in which layers of concrete and textile reinforcement are applied to moving conveyor belts and

rolled smooth. This approach is ideal for producing sheet-like products. A semicontinuous (stop-go) production method for producing more complex textile-reinforced concrete sections has been developed by the Fraunhofer Institute for Production Technology. After feeding the textile into an enclosed chamber, the concrete is injected, subsequently extruded and transported out of the chamber on a conveyor belt for hardening in a kiln. This technology is still undergoing trials.[2]

Jointing of components

Both detachable and non-detachable jointing methods may be used with textile-reinforced concrete components. The thin walls common with such components enable individual fixings such as bolts to be used. However, the holes required for such fixings essentially represent a disruption in the microstructure of this composite material and therefore are not an ideal means of jointing. Nevertheless, this method does provide a quick and easy way of erecting and dismantling textile-reinforced concrete components, especially in view of the fact that such components can only be used in the form of prefabricated elements. The efficiency of individual fixings can be considerably improved by reinforcing the holes with metal sleeves, either cast in or attached with adhesive. The non-detachable jointing methods include adhesive and grouted joints. Adhesives based on polyurethane or epoxy resins can be used to bond together the surfaces of textile-reinforced concrete components. The ambient conditions (dust, temperature, moisture) can cause problems when trying to achieve a good-quality adhesive joint, which means that good adhesive joints are hardly feasible under normal building site conditions. Furthermore, to date it has not been possible to bond together textile-reinforced concrete components in

the plane of the textile reinforcement itself, so the maximum achievable tensile strength of the joint is limited by the tensile strength of the concrete itself. Grouted joints, in which the layers of textile reinforcement in the components to be connected are left protruding from the edges and are cast in with grout, represent the most homogeneous type of joint because the microstructure is not disrupted as in the bolted joint. However, initial trials have thrown up problems with the handling of the textiles in the small grouting spaces. No data is yet available regarding the loadbearing capacity of grouted joints.[3]

Technical problems

A good bond between the textile reinforcement and the concrete is crucial for the efficiency of this composite building material. Extensive trials have shown that so far it has not been possible to activate (for loadbearing purposes) all the filaments of a roving to an adequate extent. Essentially, only the outermost filaments, i.e. those in direct contact with the concrete matrix, are activated. To accomplish better utilisation of the reinforcement, it is necessary for the fine concrete mix to achieve greater penetration of the rovings. Dispersions or synthetic resins can be used to bond together the filaments in a roving and thus activate them all for load-carrying purposes. One significant problem during the production of concrete components is how to fix the textile

1   Multiaxial net with yarns at angles of 0°, 45° and 90°
2   Spacer fabric with different spacings between the textile layers
3   Seamless textile tube
4   Multiaxial net without concrete
5   The fluid, fine concrete mix penetrates the textile reinforcement
6   Multiaxial net embedded in concrete

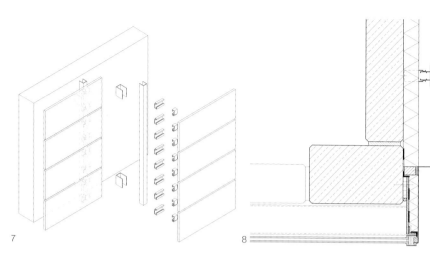

7

8

9

reinforcement in the formwork. The majority of uncoated textiles are highly flexible, which results in them dropping to the bottom of the forms, rising to float on the wet concrete, or being pressed against the sides of the formwork, all of which can have a detrimental effect on the surface finish, durability and loadbearing capacity of a component. Appropriate spacers that permit the economic production of high-quality textile-reinforced concrete components are still undergoing development. The fluid consistence of the fine concrete mix enables the production of sharp-edged components which are, however, extremely

vulnerable to mechanical damage. Such accurate edges therefore suffer during erection. Appropriate protective measures are necessary.

Applications

These days, the design of buildings is carried out bearing in mind the principle of sustainability. This addresses not only the aspect consumption while the building is in use, but also issues concerning the production and transport of the energy required, flexibility of usage, and, in the end, the recycling of structures. Considering, in particular, the aspects of

the production of a structure and the transport of its components and materials, it is advisable to work with lightweight building materials and forms of construction that save materials. This notion opens up far-reaching opportunities for textile-reinforced concrete. Slender components just 10–20 mm thick offer considerable advantages over conventional concrete precisely where the natural appearance of concrete is required, i.e. high-quality fair-face concrete surfaces on building facades and internal walls. Lightweight supporting frameworks, the reduction in thickness of external walls, simple erection and dismantling, plus the use of light-duty cranes and hoists are the principal advantages. In terms of building envelopes, the use of facade systems with a ventilated cavity as well as the use of sandwich panels – loadbearing or non-loadbearing – is conceivable. Furthermore, owing to their thin walls, textile-reinforced concrete components can also be used for secondary elements on the building envelope, e.g. sunshades. Structural systems can also benefit from the weight-savings due to the slenderness of the components – especially those systems in which the deformation of surfaces by folding or curving result in improved loadbearing capacities. Textile-reinforced concrete is ideal for such systems because the (usually) planar reinforcing textiles can be employed very effectively in such circumstances. We are speaking here primarily of folded structures, or shell structures in single or double curvature which due to intelligent form-finding – also in the sense of a low consumption of materials – represent very efficient structures. Forms of construction resolved into individual members, e.g. lattice shells (originally in timber), are also conceivable. In such cases it is the high degree of prefabrication that provides advantages over other materials such as steel or tim-

10

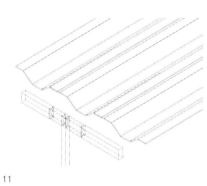

11

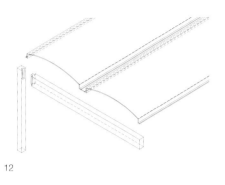

12

7   Textile-reinforced concrete facade panels on an aluminium supporting framework with retaining hooks
8, 9 Corner detail: transition from facade of textile-reinforced concrete facade panels with ventilated cavity to steel-and-glass facade
10   Part view of facade of textile-reinforced concrete facade panels with ventilated cavity, testing facility, RWTH University, Aachen; architects; Weiss + Schätzke, Aachen
     Architects: Weiss + Schätzke, Aachen
11   Folded plate roof structure made from textile-reinforced concrete
12   Barrel vault made from textile-reinforced concrete

ber. Another possible structural application, as yet little researched, is in frames of linear members made from textile-reinforced concrete sections. The initial trials involving hollow sections made from textile-reinforced concrete carried out at the Institute for Textile Engineering at the RWTH University, Aachen, Germany, and the Fraunhofer Institute for Production Technology resulted in thin-wall (5 mm) concrete circular sections with a high-quality surface finish. Together with the favourable fire behaviour that is to be expected, this opens up a completely new range of applications for concrete in building.

In terms of their overall function, the aforementioned sandwich panels represent a hybrid form comprising facade component and structural component. As an integral part of the wall they can fulfil all the building performance requirements, despite their simple layer-type construction, and at the same time provide loadbearing functions. This makes them particularly suitable for inexpensive housing and industrial buildings. Besides the building industry, manufacturers of commodity goods are also finding applications for textile-reinforced concrete. Furniture design is currently enjoying new impetus provided by this material. Here again, the weight-savings and the good surface finish of the fluid, fine concrete are very beneficial. Furthermore, subsidiary components such as integral formwork and service ducts represent other fields of application for textile-reinforced concrete.

Textile-reinforced concrete facade with ventilated cavity

Textile-reinforced concrete elements were used as a weatherproof facade with a ventilated cavity on the extension to the test facility at the Institute for Structural Concrete, RWTH University, Aachen,

Germany. The elements – flat panels just 25 mm thick with a fair-face concrete surface and overall dimensions of 2685 × 340 mm – are used to clad both the long sides of the building – a total facade area of 240 m² (fig. 10). Thanks to their low weight of 57.5 kg/m², it was possible to use a conventional supporting framework of aluminium sections and retaining hooks with four fixings per panel (fig. 7). Concealed fixings employing undercut anchors were used for the hooks on the rear of each panel. The panels are made from a high-strength fine concrete mix reinforced with an alkali-resistant glass-fibre net placed in two layers near the surface. The dimensions and concrete tensile strength are such that the panels do not crack at the serviceability limit state. This project enabled experience to be gained regarding the engineering and architectural treatment of this new material. In order to emphasize the skin-like character of the curtain wall and the slenderness of the individual panels, 15 mm wide joints separate the panels. And at the corners of the building the adjoining sheet aluminium cladding panels are set back to reveal the ends of the facade panels (figs 8 and 9). This creates an elegant transition to the glass facade. Fixed sunshading will later be added over the windows, where a series of lightweight louvres made from horizontal textile-reinforced concrete elements will break up the panel-type facade.

Stressed-skin roof structures

The thin-wall form of textile-reinforced concrete components and the, generally, planar nature of the reinforcing textiles make them especially suitable for loadbearing structures in which a deformation of the surface achieves good load-carrying capacity. Loadbearing behaviour can be optimised through folded, curved, corrugated or arch forms. In particular, a pla-

nar arrangement of the tension zone enables the development of ideal material forms – a distinct difference to conventional reinforced concrete. Initial trials and accompanying structural analyses resulted in various structural forms for small and medium spans based on planar geometries.

Folded plate beam

Even in conventional reinforced concrete, this simple beam is one of the most economic forms of construction. The combination of loadbearing beam and roof panel lead one to expect numerous potential applications; the assembly of rectangular panels would seem to make large-scale production a realistic proposition. Preliminary calculations for a material thickness of just 25 mm in textile-reinforced concrete resulted in a span of 9 m and a structural depth (rise) of 350 mm. In order to be able to accommodate the tension forces, triple carbon reinforcement with a cross-sectional area of 113 mm²/m was incorporated in the component. The longitudinal joints between the elements are at the crests of the folds and are therefore subjected to low water loads only. Simple overlapping mortar joints is a jointing principle that permits the elements to be positioned at various pitches. With a self-weight of 58 kg/m², this represents an efficient, lightweight single-storey shed system for medium spans (fig. 11).

Barrel vault

The shell effect of thin concrete structures is well suited to barrel vaults (fig. 12). This loadbearing principle represents an alternative to the simple beam action of the folded plate beam. The shell is stiff both parallel and perpendicular to the generating straight lines. A barrel vault in textile-reinforced concrete – with a material thickness of 25 mm – is therefore

13

14

very lightweight. The potential spans of up to 8 m with a structural depth (rise) of approx. 500 mm result in interesting applications for small and medium single-storey sheds. Compression forces ensue in the curved surface of the shell, tension forces in the bottom flanges of the element, which are resisted by a double layer of carbon-fibre reinforcement. On single-storey shed roofs, gutters for drainage can be incorporated along the longitudinal joints between the elements.

Arches made from diamond-shaped elements of textile-reinforced concrete
Lattice structures made from linear members represent further conceivable applications for textile-reinforced concrete (figs. 13 and 14). Unlike stressed-skin components, the cross-sectional geometry of the majority of linear members does not permit optimum positioning of the reinforcement. Structures loaded in compression, e.g. lattice shells, are therefore a good alternative.

The use of diamond-shaped lattice structures to create arches is a construction principle that has been used for single-storey sheds for the past 100 years or so. The efficiency of such systems is due, on the one hand, to the fact that small, slender individual components can be joined together to create the total structure, and on the other hand, to which the diagonal form itself provides stability in the longitudinal direction of the building without the need for any additional measures. One disadvantage is the nodes, which are often complicated: in the Zollinger method there are three linear members to connect at one point, in all other diamond-shaped lattice structures, four. Grouting of these nodes is time-consuming and expensive, and is the reason for the lack of popularity of concrete diamond-shaped lattice structures.

Textile-reinforced concrete offers other opportunities in terms of prefabrication and jointing such as bolting and bonding with adhesive, which could lead to concrete being chosen for delicate lattice structures. Diamond-shaped lattice structures can be prefabricated as slender, lightweight components. In doing so, the number of components to be joined at the nodes can be reduced to two (fig. 15). Furthermore, these thin-wall components (25 mm) also permit the use of simple bolted connections at the nodes. Smaller arches with spans from 8 to 15 m can be built using this simple method. The extremely slender textile-reinforced concrete components result in a delicate appearance that was not associated with concrete in the past. This also applies to the details. The fluid, fine concrete mix enables the formation of grooves and recesses for fasteners, which leads to elegant joints. The first prototype of such an arch made from diamond-shaped elements was built at the RWTH University, Aachen, Germany, within the scope of a

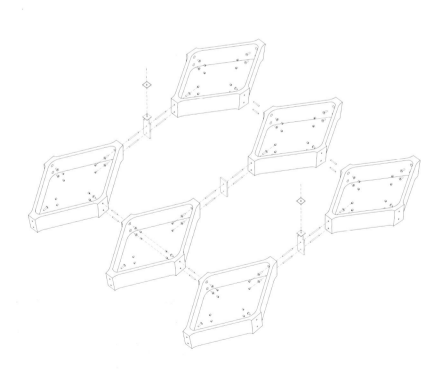

15

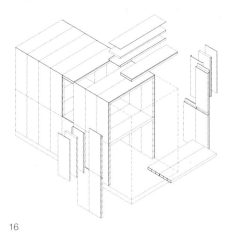

16

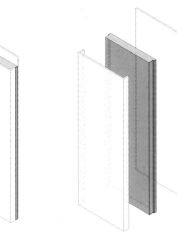

17

18

special research project. The individual diamond-shaped elements are reinforced with two layers of carbon-fibre nets. Stainless steel sleeves cast in at the corners of the elements are used for fixing the reinforcement and for the close-tolerance connections between the elements. A 5° bevel on the narrow sides results in a polygonal arch structure in addition to the diamond-shaped elements.

Integral components
In other applications as well, e.g. housing, the use of textile-reinforced concrete for roof and floor structures seems possible. Owing to the type of usage, shorter spans of 3–5 m should be assumed and components with simple, orthogonal geometries. Sandwich technology would appear to be the right approach in order to achieve the necessary load-carrying capacity and at the same time satisfy the high building performance demands (especially thermal insulation). The fabrication of slender sandwich components comprising two textile-reinforced concrete facings (with a high-quality finish) and a core of insulating material (expanded polyurethane foam) increases the stiffness of the overall component. This permits the use of such panels for loadbearing wall, floor and roof elements in one and two-storey buildings, but still requires further research into the building performance properties such as sound insulation, moisture control, vapour diffusion and behaviour in fire. A house based on this system is the subject of a current development project in which the full building performance functionality is still possible with small component cross-sections and high-quality fair-face concrete surfaces. The extremely simple construction of the wall and roof elements envisaged would consist of 15 mm textile-reinforced concrete facings inside and outside plus an insulating core of expanded

foam. Owing to the high compressive strength of the concrete, the vertical loads can be carried via the inner facing of the sandwich component. The higher loads on the floor elements require the provision of webs between the two facings. Prototype hollow box beam-like floor elements have already been produced. Besides a further increase in their load-carrying capacity, it is the development of the joints between such sandwich elements that represents one focus in the ongoing research.

References:

[1] Hegger, Josef, et al.: Fassaden aus textilbewehrtem Beton; in: Beton- und Fertigteiljahrbuch 2005, vol. 53, pp. 76–82
[2] Hegger, Josef, et al.: Neue Bauteile aus textilbewehrtem Beton; in: Beton und Stahlbetonbau, No. 6, 2004, pp. 68–71
[3] Sedlacek, Gerhard, et al.: Fügen von Bauteilen aus textilbewehrtem Beton; in: Bauingenieur, No. 12, 2004, pp. 569–75

13, 14 Diamond-shaped lattice arch made from textile-reinforced concrete, temporary assembly for demonstration purposes, Aachen, February 2005: design: Chair of Building Construction 2, RWTH University, Aachen
15   Joints between textile-reinforced concrete elements with integral facade connections, isometric view
16   System building with textile-reinforced sandwich components, schematic isometric view
17   Schematic construction of a wall element
18   Hollow box beam element for floors, prototype

Lightweight wood particle concrete – properties and potential applications

Roland Krippner

1   Making a functional model with glass-fibre cloth reinforcement
2   Averaged values for the specific heat capacity and thermal conductivity of lightweight wood particle concrete
3   Comparison of the moisture absorption behaviour of plywood (blue and red) and lightweight wood particle concrete "light" (orange and green)

The specific properties of wood make it suitable for diverse applications in building. Besides the well-known engineering and architectural uses, this regenerative material can also be employed in the form of chips, e.g. in combination with hydraulic or mineral binders, for high-quality building products. This technology results in ecologically and economically sensible utilisation of the woodworking industry's waste materials, enabling the recycling requirements of a construction without depletion cradle-to-grave economy to be met.

What is lightweight wood particle concrete?
Lightweight wood particle concrete is a composite material made from cement, wood chips, water and additives. Depending on the particular mix of these ingredients, densities between 400 and 1700 kg/m³ are possible. This places the material in the lightweight concrete category of DIN EN 206-1. However, the standard does not consider organic aggregates, only rock aggregates. Consequently, this material is not covered by the standard and there are no other standards dealing with the use of wood residues as an aggregate for concrete instead of gravel and sand. As a rule, building authority approval would be required for every project.
Lightweight wood particle concrete contains about < 25 % by mass crushed wood chips or sawdust, about < 65 % by mass hydraulic binder, and water plus, if applicable, further additives.
The woodworking industry produces shavings, chips and sawdust in great quantities – wastes and residues that can be used beneficially by mixing with cement and water. The demand for the re-use of residues is an important factor in promoting sustainable construction without depletion of resources.

History of the material
The combination of inorganic building materials with wood residues from the woodworking industry is not a new development: indeed, it can be traced back to the early 20th century. Names such as flooring cement, cement-wood floor and wood particle concrete designate a series of concrete types that were used primarily as screeds and renders. Flooring cement is regarded as pleasantly warm underfoot and was widely used in housing until the 1950s. It was also used in many famous projects of the modern movement, including the Bauhaus building in Dessau, Stuttgart's Weissenhof Estate and the Van Nelle factory in Rotterdam.[1]

The granting of patents for relevant methods in the early 1930s paved the way for the production of "wood chip concrete". After the Second World War the lack of raw materials gave rise to experiments with cement-bonded wood-based products. And in the late 1960s this approach was taken up with vigour in the former GDR. To simplify handling, wood particle concrete was processed in the form of small-format panels and bricks for (loadbearing) internal and external walls in small apartments and agricultural buildings.[2]

If we consider the diverse approaches and products, it is easy to compile a list of the advantages for this combination of materials:

· good thermal insulation properties and high elasticity
· resistance to abrasion
· good sorption ability
· agreeable surface temperatures

The disadvantages are the high shrinkage and swelling, and in flooring cement the tendency to crack plus – depending on the mineralisation process – possible corrosion problems for any embedded metal reinforcement.

Embracing the ideas of sparing resources (sand, gravel) and saving weight (wall and floor assemblies), these concepts have been re-explored in recent years and developed further using current technological possibilities. Although components based on a mixture of cement, wood and water are these days used essentially only as pressed, cement-bonded particleboards or as lightweight wood-wool slabs for non-loadbearing, thermal insulation functions, the ongoing development of this combination of materials offers promising opportunities for the building industry in general. Moreover, wood chip, or rather lightweight wood particle, concrete with its natural ingredients and its "complete" recycling chain is gaining in importance in the course of the re-evaluation of energy and materials flows.

Lightweight wood particle concrete as a material for external walls

Munich's Technical University has been carrying out investigations into the potential uses of lightweight wood particle concrete for building facades [4] on three mutually supportive fronts: lightweight wood particle concrete as a material for thermally passive and thermally active components, plus lightweight wood particle concrete in combination with phase change materials (PCM). This involved extensive tests and experiments, forecasts and functional models at different scales (fig. 1).

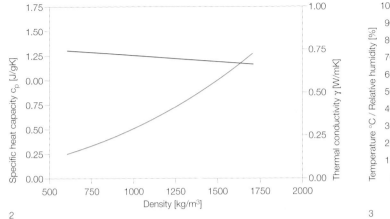

2

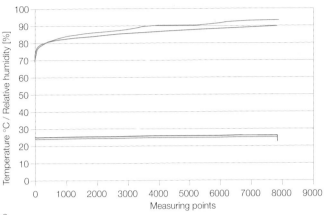

3

Building construction properties
The difference between conventional timber products, wood-based products and lightweight wood particle concrete is the latter's higher density, its brittle failure behaviour and its lower moisture-related change in length. Lightweight wood particle concrete is characterised by its processing properties: it can be mixed easily manually or with customary plant; sawing, nailing and screwing are possible. There are also numerous options for finishing the surface (see figs 8a–f).
Compared to normal-weight concrete, lightweight wood particle concrete is characterised by a higher binder content and also a higher water/cement ratio. As it shows no tendency to segregate, it can be placed by pouring, pumping or tipping depending on consistence – just like lightweight concretes.
The water/cement ratio (optimum between 0.55 and 0.65, see also p. 22) and the wood/cement ratio (compressive and tensile strengths rise with the proportion of cement) are the main factors affecting strength and workability. Mixes with densities > 1300 kg/m³ and cement contents > 800 kg/m³ can produce compressive strengths of up to 13 N/mm² and moduli of elasticity of up to 5000 N/mm². As any metal embedded in lightweight wood particle concrete is likely to corrode, and there is also a demand to reduce weight and optimise cross-sections, steel meshes or bars with spacers are not suitable for reinforcing lightweight wood particle concrete. Textiles represent efficient and cost-effective alternatives – as revealed by intensive research work into modern methods of reinforcement for concrete [5] (see "Textile-reinforced concrete", pp. 32–37).

Building performance properties
As a hygroscopic, vapour-permeable building material, lightweight wood particle concrete exhibits good thermal behaviour in terms of both thermal insulation and heat storage capacity. Both are heavily dependent on the density of the material. Lightweight wood particle concrete assemblies can therefore contribute effectively to overheating protection in summer and thermal insulation in winter thanks to the good variability of the mixing ratios.
Investigations into the thermal conductivity resulted in values from 0.15 W/mK (ρ = 600 kg/m³) to 0.75 W/mK (ρ = 1700 kg/m³) (fig. 2). In terms of its insulating effect, this places the material in the region of aerated concrete and lightweight concretes with a no-fines microstructure. Rough calculations reveal a marketable potential for thermally passive external wall components with multi-layer wall assemblies (d ≤ 300 mm, U-values between 0.45 and 0.28 W/m²K). The results of building simulations show that the standard of conventional clay brickwork construction (1995 German Thermal Insulation Act) is at least reached and in some cases the heating energy requirement can be reduced by 15–20%. However, the wall assemblies tested so far have not achieved values in the range of low-energy forms of construction.
The specific heat capacity of lightweight wood particle concrete (0.9–1.5 J/gK) lies between that of clay brickwork or concrete and man-made foam or natural fibre insulating material. The volume-related heat capacity (0.39–0.48/ρ = 1250 kg/m³) is about 60–70% that of normal-weight concrete.
Trials with solid absorbers made from lightweight wood particle concrete, however, revealed only a limited potential. Despite the relatively high volume-related heat storage capacity of lightweight wood

particle concrete (ρ = 1250 kg/m³), this did not become effective for the thermal behaviour under the chosen boundary conditions. In the light of the fundamental problem of solar energy – the disparity between demand and availability – and the fact that with a high availability of solar radiation the heating requirement is already reduced through passive solar energy gains, the potential of the solid absorber system remains limited. Nevertheless, good data is available for further investigations into the potential applications of lightweight wood particle concrete in thermally active components for temperature equalisation of building components.[6]
Good airborne and impact sound insulation can be achieved by varying the density or using multi-layer forms of construction. Sound transmissions via joints and leaks in the building envelope can be overcome by using grouted joints and careful detailing.
Lightweight wood particle concrete is incombustible and thicknesses ≥ 50 mm achieve a fire resistance of 90 minutes.

The building construction and building performance properties show that lightweight wood particle concrete can compete with conventional building materials in the marketplace for external wall materials. A simplified, rough calculation reveals that lightweight wood particle concrete is about 30% more expensive than normal-weight concrete. This is primarily due to the increased binder content and the, at present, low prices for normal aggregates.
However, in terms of its marketing potential, lightweight wood particle concrete should be seen as a rival to lightweight concretes in which high-strength substances such as expanded clay etc. are generally used. Comparisons with this group of materials reveal cost advan-

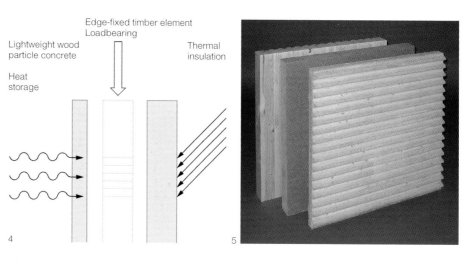

tages of 30–40 % because the wood content represents a readily available, low-cost waste product.[7]
Like other timber and wood-based products, the primary energy requirement for manufacture, transport and erection is low, provided the raw materials are obtained locally.[8] The material is easy to transport, and is also easy to demolish, dismantle and re-use for the production of new building components.

Lightweight wood particle concrete with phase change materials

One particular problem with lightweight structures is the rapid heating and cooling effects owing to the lack of storage capacity. These fluctuations can severely impair the comfort for users and – when these are smoothed out by using additional cooling or heating systems – to increased energy consumption.

The task of temporarily storing excessive thermal energy for releasing into the interior at a later time calls for materials with high admittance (i.e. energy storage density). In this context, phase change materials (PCM), with their ability to store large quantities of heat within a narrow temperature range, represent a promising new avenue for building materials.[10] It is precisely this combination that opens up new development opportunities for the use of lightweight wood particle concrete. The comprehensive trials surrounding the combination of lightweight wood particle concrete and organic PCMs (based on paraffin) achieved densities of 1000–1450 kg/m^3 (wood: 6–17 % by mass; PCM: 11–29 % by mass). As the PCM is three times heavier than wood, changes to the strength values were to be expected. Investigations into the compressive strength revealed higher values (up to 20 N/mm^2) than "normal" lightweight wood particle concrete. Furthermore, it was mainly the modulus of

elasticity measurements that indicated a very homogeneous composite material despite the disparity of the raw materials. Freeze–thaw cycle tests revealed a good frost resistance. And very good durability is guaranteed owing to the material's elastomechanical properties, even with high w/c ratios.
On the whole, good building construction parameters were achieved for building facades and interiors.

The building performance studies confirmed the suitability of this material for both internal and external applications. The thermal conductivity (ρ-values between 0.28 and 0.50 W/mK) for higher densities lies below that of the original lightweight wood particle concrete. The heat storage capacity (fig. 2) and the moisture equilibrium behaviour represent further advantages.

Experiments concerning the moisture equilibrium behaviour of lightweight wood particle concrete also supplied good results. For example, this material is only marginally inferior to plywood (fig. 3).[11] Lightweight wood particle concrete with its stabilising effect (i.e. reducing the fluctuations in the relative humidity of the air, or buffering the moisture peaks that can occur in wet interior areas) can help to regulate an internal climate regarded as agreeable. This has an effect on the ventilation of buildings: smaller ventilation systems can be installed and that will bring significant energy and cost-savings. The thermal and moisture properties, in conjunction with the acoustic requirements for the materials used for internal floors, walls and soffits, are important parameters which help to ensure a comfortable internal climate. In addition, the surface finishes also influence the "visual" comfort. And wood is regarded as a good light modulator, especially in daylight.

A homogeneous colour spectrum can be expected from lightweight wood particle concrete surfaces, which will have a positive influence on the internal lighting conditions.

The first fire tests in a small furnace resulted in good fire resistance figures. However, the combination of lightweight wood particle concrete and phase change materials will probably not achieve German building materials class A 2 (incombustible, but containing combustible materials).

An appraisal of the potential reveals that – with efficient passive ventilation and cooling strategies – this composite material achieves a significant reduction in the number of hours of overheating in an office. And if the heat storage capacity can be further enhanced by using phase change materials, the protection against overheating in summer can be improved still further.[12] These results are similar to those from investigations into other building materials containing PCMs.

Lightweight wood particle concrete–solid timber composite construction

During the investigations into the material itself, work was carried out to establish the principles for external wall assemblies using lightweight wood particle concrete in conjunction with solid timber.

Lightweight wood particle concrete and solid timber forms of construction
Lightweight wood particle concrete–solid timber composite construction embodies a (further) development potential for both innovative timber and concrete construction.[13] Such composite forms of construction substantially improve the structural and acoustic properties of floor and wall components. The no-voids assembly results in:

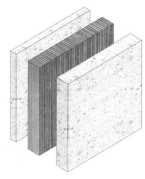

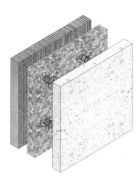

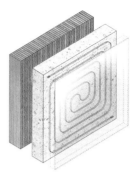

6a

b

c

- better heat storage capacity
- balanced moisture behaviour
- exclusion of "internal" fire propagation

Besides weather and fire protection, composite forms of construction exhibit many advantages in terms of production:

- high degree of prefabrication
- low weight
- simple transport
- fast erection

Both solid timber products and lightweight wood particle concrete open up diverse engineering and architectural opportunities. In doing so, the combination of efficient composite materials and innovative production plays a fundamental role in the development of well-devised building (component) systems.

Assemblies and layers
In the wall assemblies conceived, there is a functional separation between the load-bearing, thermal insulation and heat storage layers (fig. 4). When lightweight wood particle concrete is used as a structural component (ρ > 1500 kg/m³), the wood content is well below 10% by mass. As the density increases, so does the thermal conductivity, and the thermal insulation effect drops markedly. Therefore, a solid layer of timber – in the following examples an edge-fixed element – must be provided to carry the loads. In doing so, the advantages of solid timber construction, i.e. the ability to accommodate considerable vertical and horizontal actions, can be exploited.
In these wall assemblies the lightweight wood particle concrete becomes a passive component providing thermal insulation and heat storage functions. It can also be used as a thermally active component to back up the hot water or cooling requirements.

Lightweight wood particle concrete can be used in multi-leaf and/or multi-layer forms of construction with conventional ventilated (timber) cladding acting as weather protection or an interior lining. Depending on requirements, e.g. when being used as a thermally active component, the assemblies can be covered with glass or transparent thermal insulation or translucent materials such as polycarbonate panels (figs 5 and 6a–c).

Potential applications
A broad range of possible primary structure applications is envisaged for composite components of solid timber and lightweight wood particle concrete, especially in housing and office buildings. Owing to its versatile material properties, lightweight wood particle concrete in diverse combinations is suitable for use in the form of prefabricated components but also for in situ concrete. Furthermore, wall and floor elements can be produced for both internal and external applications. Despite its porous structure, this composite material exhibits good weathering resistance. In addition, the organic, fine-grain wood chips can give rise to aesthetically attractive surface finishes, which can be emphasized by using further additives. This makes lightweight wood particle concrete particularly suitable for exposed applications.

Surface finishes
Surface textures and treatments represent key criteria when selecting building materials intended for use in exposed places on facades or interior walls. The first thing we notice about lightweight wood particle concrete is that its organic constituents on the whole lead to a "warmer" general colouring compared to building materials with a pure mineral content. Moreover, the wood particles are very well distributed over all surfaces,

partly due to their relatively small particle size (4 mm) (figs 8a–f). The porous microstructure of lightweight wood particle concrete restricts the choice of surface treatment options. The surfaces were initially sawn and ground within the scope of the trials. The wood particles and PCM granulate dominate the appearance of the ensuing cut surfaces, which remind the observer of reddish-yellow to grey-yellow natural stone.

Colours and textured formwork
There are interesting, diverse possibilities for colouring lightweight wood particle concrete. The liquid paints in red and yellow used during the trials represent inexpensive, readily available additives which also reflect the specific colouring of the lightweight wood particle concrete and the species of wood used. The stronger accentuation of a certain proportion of wood can be recognised by the increase in the colour saturation. Yellow colours allow the wood particles to retreat into the background somewhat, whereas the PCM granulate is emphasized. The result is reversed with red. Despite this effect, the constituent materials do not take on a uniform appearance. Where it is cut through, the PCM granulate exhibits many diverse nuances of colour, and the wood, too, remains visible in both colorations.

4   Functional layers of lightweight wood particle concrete–solid timber composite construction
5   "External wall building kit" (600 × 600 mm): 3-layer assembly, edge-fixed timber element + extra insulation + "corrugated" lightweight wood particle concrete (outside)
6   Concepts for external wall assemblies using lightweight wood particle concrete:
   a   3-layer assembly, lightweight wood particle concrete (inside) + edge-fixed timber element + lightweight wood particle concrete (outside)
   b   3-layer assembly, edge-fixed timber element + extra insulation + lightweight wood particle concrete (outside)
   c   3-layer assembly, edge-fixed timber element + lightweight wood particle concrete (e.g.) as solid absorber + glass covering (outside)

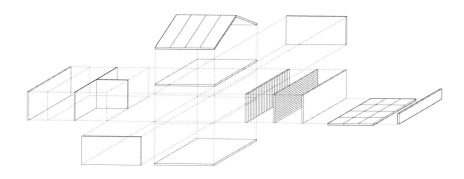

7

There are also numerous options for adding texture to the surface. However, the use of form liners or finely textured plastic forms requires a higher content of ultra-fine constituents near the surface of the lightweight wood particle concrete. Owing to the material's porous micro-structure, lightweight mixes in particular require more elaborate compaction measures when placing the concrete in the formwork, and the use of additives when very dense surfaces are required.

Use of plasticisers
The use of building chemicals to improve, in particular, the wet concrete properties of lightweight wood particle concrete is to be expected in the production of fair-face concrete surfaces with a dense structure and to reduce the amount of water required.
However, the example of plasticisers illustrates that the use of concrete additives places special demands on the wood/cement/water mix. The influence of the w/c ratio and the mixing time on the effect of plasticisers will need to be carefully checked in further trials.

Concluding remarks and outlook
Extensive research activities are taking place in the field of concrete technology. Three areas are especially relevant for building. Besides self-compacting and high-strength (structural lightweight) concretes, the combination with corrosion-resistant textile fibres as a reinforcing material is gaining in importance. Furthermore, current research work is primarily characterised by the greater use of building chemicals.
In the case of lightweight wood particle concrete, the development objectives are, on the one hand, better utilisation of the wood (i.e. the use of low-strength wood and wood residues), and on the other, the optimisation of building construction and building performance parameters while retaining the positive properties of the wood.
Lightweight wood particle concrete is a rediscovered material whose building construction and building performance properties and potential applications for building have not yet been fully investigated. Owing to the very nature of timber and concrete, they exhibit different

advantages and disadvantages. They tend to be competitors in some areas of construction (walls, floors). But in composite forms of construction in particular, numerous synergy effects can be achieved through the sensible use of the positive properties of both materials.

These aspects formed the "programmatic" background to a design for a high-rise block in Zürich, which was developed within the scope of a planning report and presented at the Swiss Federal Institute of Technology in Zürich. It is a resources-saving form of construction involving extensive use of timber. The concept provides for a primary loadbearing structure of steel with floors of precast concrete elements. Units with up to three storeys – for residential and commercial uses – are positioned in these horizontal fire compartments. Their loadbearing and enclosing elements are made from timber or a lightweight wood particle concrete–solid timber composite construction (fig. 9).

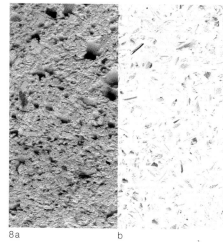
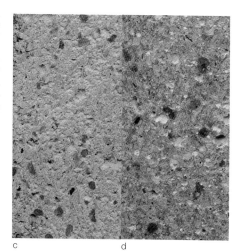
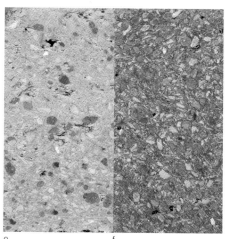

8a   b   c   d   e   f

9

Despite the experiences gained and the knowledge about many parameters, there is still a need to optimise this material, especially with regard to the mix ratios, processing methods and the use of textile reinforcement. Further detailed research work on the constructional behaviour and production technology aspects are required before large-format prefabricated elements of lightweight wood particle concrete can be used in buildings. That work includes:

• the form of the wood constituents
• the behaviour with other types of cement
• the way additives influence workability

Furthermore, lightweight wood particle concrete–solid timber composite construction will require investigations into fixings and fasteners. Other important work concerns the assessment of lightweight wood particle concrete in terms of its sustainability, the potential savings with respect to mineral raw materials and its recyclability.
The findings already available represent the essential material properties and functional models at the "laboratory scale" for a sort of external wall building kit. The next step in the product development will be experiments linked to production technology and building construction issues, and the construction of full-size models, which is currently being carried out at Munich Technical University within the scope of a joint research project.[14]
Owing to its positive properties, lightweight wood particle concrete can be regarded as a forward-looking, efficient material, especially for thermally passive components. The combination with PCM offers further functional and constructional advantages, primarily in the field of building without depleting resources,

which means lighter and thinner wall elements with, at the same time, better thermodynamic material properties.
Furthermore, lightweight wood particle concrete opens up a series of interesting architectural options for floor coverings plus wall, floor and soffit finishes.

References:

[1] Lietz, Bettina; Markgraf, Monika: Architekturober-flächen. Bauhausbauten Dessau – Fußböden; pub. by Stiftung Bauhaus Dessau, Dessau 2004, pp. 19–27
[2] Bursian, Gerolf; Pinternagel, Ernst-Karl: Holz-beton. Produktion, Anwendung und Erfahrungen; Schriftenreihen der Bauforschung; vol. 20, Berlin, 1973
[3] Beraus, Erich: Holzspanbeton. Naturbaustoff – ökologisch und wirtschaftlich; in: Beton + Fertig-teil Jahrbuch 2001, Wiesbaden, 2001, p. 104f.
[4] Within the scope of a dissertation and further, ongoing, parallel R&D projects at the Chair of Building Technology (Prof. Thomas Herzog); the investigations into lightweight wood particle concrete by Prof. Julius Natterer at the EPF in Lausanne (I-Bois, Institute of Timber Construction) formed the starting point for the work.
[5] Hegger, Josef; Will, Norbert: Bauteile aus textil-bewehrtem Beton; in: DBZ – Deutsche Bauzeit-schrift 4/2003, pp. 68–71, and Gliniorz, Kai-Uwe; Natterer, Julius: Formbauteile aus Holzleicht-beton, final report, KTI Project 3497.1, Lausanne, 2000, pp. 90–131
[6] Krippner, Roland: Zu Einsatzmöglichkeiten von Holzleichtbeton im Bereich von Gebäudefassa-den, dissertation, Munich: Munich Technical University, Chair of Building Technology, May 2004, pp. 61–78 http://tumb1.biblio.tu-muenchen.de/publ/diss/ar/2004/krippner.html
[7] Cost estimate for Switzerland in 2000; cf. Glin-iorz/Natterer, pp. 87ff. (see [5])
[8] Sambeth, Burkhard M.: Holz- und Holzwerkstoffe; in: Haefele, Gottfried, et al. (ed.): Baustoffe und Ökologie, Tübingen, 1996, pp. 158–83
[9] The use of timber in construction is today only about one-tenth of the volume of that used in around 1900.
[10] Mehling, Harald: Latentwärmespeicher. BINE In-formationsdienst; themeninfo IV/02; Eggenstein-Leopoldshafen 2002, and Pfafferott, Jens: Passive Kühlung mit Nachtlüftung. BINE Infor-mationsdienst; themeninfo I/03, Eggenstein-Leopoldshafen, 2003
[11] Carried out by Delzer Kybernetik in Lörrach using "static" and "dynamic" measuring techniques.
[12] Krippner, Roland: Untersuchungen zu Einsatz-möglichkeiten von Holzleichtbeton mit Latent-wärmespeichermaterialien; in: Bauphysik 3/2005, pp. 173–80
[13] Krippner, Roland: Holzleichtbeton im Bereich von Gebäudefassaden; in: Deutscher Holzbau-preis 2005, Informationsdienst Holz, 05/2005, p. 41
[14] At the Chair of Construction and Building Materials, Prof. Florian Musso, within the Bava-rian "High-Tech Offensive", Upper Bavaria Regional Projects, grant applications "Holzbau der Zukunft", http://portal.mytum.de/pressestelle/pressemitteilungen/news_article.2005–05–13.2172690315 <04.08.2005>

7 Applications for lightweight wood particle concrete in building generally and residential outdoor uses
8 Different surface finishes of lightweight wood particle concrete and lightweight wood particle concrete in conjunction with phase change materials
  a Lightweight wood particle concrete
  b Lightweight wood particle concrete with white cement
  c Lightweight wood particle concrete with PCM, light mix
  d Lightweight wood particle concrete with PCM, heavy mix
  e Lightweight wood particle concrete and PCM, pigmented, 5% yellow
  f Lightweight wood particle concrete and PCM, pigmented, 5% red
9 High-rise building with extensive use of timber, south facade, planning report for Zürich, 2002; architects: Thomas Herzog, with Matthias Sieveke

1

Sustainabilty and recycling

Peter Lieblang

Energy-efficient building with concrete
About 40% of the total primary energy requirement in the European Union can be attributed to buildings. On 16 December 2002 the European Parliament therefore passed the Energy Performance of Buildings Directive (EPBD) with the aim of reducing this energy consumption drastically. This directive must be implemented in the national legislation of every EU member state by 4 January 2006. In Germany the Energy Economy Act, which fulfils many of the requirements of the European directive, has been in force since February 2002. The significance of the heat storage capacity of components and structures plays a greater role in the calculation of the primary energy requirement than was the case in the past. Limiting the energy requirements for heating and cooling buildings is the most important goal of the EPBD. The limiting values must be specified at national level, purely for reasons of climatic differences, although the assessment of the energy efficiency of buildings must be carried out based on a prognosis method standardised for the whole of Europe. In order to guarantee this, the European Committee for Standardisation (CEN) was appointed by the European commission to draw up standards for a uniform method of predicting the energy requirements of buildings. The timetable and targets of this method are described in the "Umbrella Document". There are four points directly related to the method of calculation:
· heating requirement
· heating energy requirement
· primary energy requirement and carbon dioxide emissions
· presentation of energy efficiency and limiting values

The heating and heating energy requirements are determined solely by the building, whereas the primary energy require-ment and the total energy efficiency are also influenced by the plant and systems used. Compared to the Energy Economy Act currently applicable in Germany, which besides the monthly balance method also permits a simplified analysis using the heating period as the basis for calculations, the EPBD calls for a monthly or hourly balance. The heart of this will be the new EN ISO 13790. Other standards regulate, for example, the calculation of U-values, ventilation systems or climatic boundary conditions.

Fig. 2 lists important properties of cement-bonded building materials. It is true for all building materials that the thermal conductivity and the specific heat capacity increase with the density. Up until now, energy-efficient building was equated with the use of good thermal insulation, but in future the heat storage capacity will be equally important.
The form of construction of buildings built either completely or mainly of cement-bonded building materials is often referred to as solid or monolithic construction. Contrasting with this are the lightweight forms of construction, e.g. timber or timber studding.

The properties of buildings made from cement-bonded building materials were investigated in comparative studies for different climatic regions. In comparison to buildings erected using lightweight forms of construction, the heating require-ment was about 2–8% lower, which can be primarily attributed to the greater heat storage capacity of solid building materials. Depending on the plant and systems used, this results in a primary energy saving of 3–12 kWh/m²a (fig. 3). In hot regions with a high level of solar radiation, the potential savings can be correspondingly higher. In spring and autumn in particular, owing to their relatively high spe-cific heat capacity, concrete components store the solar energy with only a moderate rise in the temperature of the component itself, which prevents uncomfortable interior temperatures. In Central Europe, this buffer effect means that one or two cooler days can be accepted without having to input heating energy.

The implementation of the EPBD will mean paying more attention to the thermal capacity of components and materials with respect to preventing overheating in summer. The specific heat capacity of solid building materials generally means that air-conditioning systems are indispensable. The cooling energy require-ment of buildings with a high thermal capacity is about 15–20% below that of buildings employing lightweight forms of construction. A series of examples reveals that the night-time ventilation is adequate to lower the temperatures of the components to such an extent that a maximum room temperature of 26°C can be maintained even on summer days with a large amount of solar radiation.
The planned switchover to a monthly or hourly balance makes this influence obvious. Owing to their high density, cement-bonded solid building materials exhibit very good heat storage capacities. At the same time, the thermal conductivity of such building materials can be minimised by using thermal insulation. The outcome is that this combination of storage capacity and insulation leads to a primary energy saving of approx. 3% compared to buildings employing lightweight forms of construction.
Particularly interesting here is the use of solid building materials above roof spaces. Although the theoretical analyses describe the energy-related quality of the entire building, they cannot exclude a high temperature rise beneath "lightweight" timber constructions during peri-

45

Important properties of cement-bonded building materials

Property		Normal-weight concr. C 20/25	Dense lightweight concr. LC 20/22	Masonry of lightweight concrete hollow blocks (2K-Hbl 2–0.6; d = 24 cm)
Density δ [kg/m³]		2400	800–1000	600
Thermal conduct. λ [W/(mK)]		2	0,49	0.32 (0.26 with LM)
Specific heat cap. c	[J/(kgK)]	1000	1000	1000
	[MJ/(m³K)]	2400	1000	600
Diffusion resistance index [–]		70–150	70–150	5–10
Perm.. compress. stress [Mpa]		$f_{cd} = 11$	$f_{cd} = 11$	perm. $\sigma_0 = 0.5$

2

1 Demolition of the "Ahornblatt" restaurant in Berlin (p. 44)
3 Heating requirements for buildings with different forms of construction in various climatic zones

ods of extremely hot weather. A solid roof construction, e.g. precast concrete elements, creates interior climate conditions in roof spaces that are almost identical to those of the storeys below.

The ecology of mineral raw materials for cement and concrete production
About 770 million tonnes of mineral materials are produced in Germany annually, with a slight yet discernible decline. The majority of these materials are used in the building industry. There tends to be a regional concentration of the extraction/ mining of these raw materials in line with the geological formations. The reserves are large enough to cover requirements – provided consumption remains stable – for several centuries.[1] Nevertheless, the deposits approved for individual extraction/mining operations frequently suffice for no more than a few years because approval for the expansion of such works often conflicts with alternative interests competing for the use of the land, e.g. natural waters or conservation areas, housing developments, agriculture. In contrast to the extraction/mining of energy media, e.g. oil, the consumption of resources in the production of mineral raw materials is, in the first place, a question of claiming areas of nature, where a decision has to be made between the different land uses all competing for recognition.
A fact often overlooked here is that the extraction of minerals represents a temporary measure with a constant claim to an area of land. For example, the quarrying of raw materials for cement production claims only 0.0002% of the land annually.[2] The restoration work that takes place once deposits are depleted forms an integral component of every quarrying operation and is stipulated in the approval documents.

The movement of materials caused by the production of cement and concrete in Germany amounts to about 45 million tonnes of limestone, marl and chalk for the production of about 35 million tonnes of cement clinker and about 130 million tonnes of aggregates (gravel and sand) every year. The lion's share of this is used for buildings. Further customers for aggregates are the manufacturers of concrete goods (about 20 million tonnes) and manufactures of concrete items for civil engineering (about 25 million tonnes).
As the mineral raw materials in a structure normally remain in place for a very long period (> 50 years), the consumption of materials accumulates in the building stock over long periods of time. It has been calculated that approx. 3.6 billion m³ of concrete has been cast since 1950, most of which is still present in the existing building stock.[3] It is probably true to say that the amount of material in buildings and structures reached its zenith around the year 2000 and since then has been slowly declining owing to more slender forms of construction and a higher proportion of dry construction techniques.

The quarrying of the raw materials and the transportation required to supply the customers are especially important when considering the ecological issues in connection with the production of mineral building materials.

When assessing the ecological aspects, it is advantageous that the transport of these materials is usually only economic over short distances. For example, the locations of the German cement industry are distributed relatively evenly across the country, corresponding to the geological deposits. This is true to an even greater extent for the quarrying of aggregates. Mineral building materials are therefore almost always regional products.

The re-use and disposal of mineral building materials also meet the demands of sustainability and ecology. The material residues generated during the demolition and dismantling of buildings and structures often supply the raw materials for the production of new, high-quality building materials. The total of mineral building debris, old pavements and building site waste in 2000 was about 90 million tonnes, but of this figure, more than 80 million tonnes of materials were recovered and recycled.[4] Although the building industry consumes huge quantities of materials in comparison to other industries, the proportion of the total annual volume of waste amounting to 400 million tonnes is amazingly small.

The current legal situation is forcing research and technology in the building industry to guarantee high-quality re-uses for the wastes and residues generated. For example, after appropriate treatment, concrete from demolition works can be used as recycled aggregate for producing new concrete. In Germany the consumption of recycled aggregate in concrete is currently about 1.5 million tonnes annually and therefore accounts for about 1.2 % of the total quantity of aggregate in concrete. It should be remembered here that the regulations covering the use of recycled aggregate were first published in 1998 and updated in 2004. The high-quality re-use of scrap concrete as aggregate for new concrete has therefore only been sanctioned by the building authorities for a few years.
Scrap concrete is recycled by treating concrete from demolition works directly. This is crushed and divided into concrete chippings and crushed fine aggregate. According to current building regulations, up to 35 % by vol. of the coarse aggregate and up to 7 % by vol. of the fine aggregate can be replaced by recycled materials.

| Region | Heating requirements | | Monthly average temp. |
	Solid construction [kWh/(m²a)]	Lightweight constr. [kWh/(m²a)]	October to April [°C]
Arctic Circle	128.7	133.4	-7.9
Northern Europe	66.7	70.7	1.1
Northern Europe/Coast	53.1	57.4	3.4
British Isles	37.6	43.1	5.9
Benelux	42.2	48.8	5.6
Central Europe	49.2	53.3	3.8
Alps	60.6	65.9	1.4
Mediterranean	8.0	12.2	12.1

3

Besides scrap concrete, any wet concrete not used on the building site can also be reused. The recycling of wet concrete forms an internal product lifecycle within the ready-mixed concrete works and involves only a relatively small quantity. Any wet concrete that is returned to the works in the truck mixers or residues left after cleaning mixers and pumps is divided into its constituent materials and fed back into the production. These recycled materials account for approx. 2.5 % of the total production of a ready-mixed concrete works. The water used for cleaning plant can also be used as mixing water. The complete reuse of all materials from the residual concrete replaces the corresponding quantities of primary raw materials. The use of residual water, residual concrete and residual mortar in the production of concrete is specified in standards and approved by the building authorities. Whether recycled aggregate can be used depends on the properties of the concrete required for the respective component. The applications for recycled aggregate can be subdivided as follows:

- as a substitute for natural aggregates in concrete according to DIN EN 206-1 based on the directive on concrete with recycled aggregates published by the German Reinforced Concrete Committee (DafStb)
- as a substitute for primary raw materials in the production of masonry units of lightweight concrete
- for direct use in roads and paths
- for direct use in the form of crushed fine aggregate in mortar for masonry
- for direct use in concrete not covered by European standard EN 206, e.g. in gardening and landscaping works or for ancillary components

The highest technical demands are placed on recycled aggregate when used in loadbearing concrete components to DIN EN 206-1 and DIN 1045. The maximum amounts that may be used according to the current regulations (35 % coarse aggregate, 7 % fine aggregate) do not impair the properties of the wet or hardened concrete. The use of recycled aggregate can in some cases require a marginally higher quantity of water owing to the porous and hence absorbent nature of the material. This is achieved, for example, by pre-wetting and using plasticisers, even for lightweight concrete. Up to compressive strength class C 30/37, the mechanical properties of the hardened concrete (compressive/tensile strength, modulus of elasticity, creepage and shrinkage) correspond to those of conventional normal-weight concrete. At higher stresses, recycled aggregate can affect the deformation behaviour of the hardened concrete. Therefore, it may not be used, for example, in prestressed concrete components or in the production of high-performance concretes (e.g. self-compacting or high-strength concrete).

Concrete is a purely mineral building material which in terms of production and usage conditions, and also in the interaction with its environment, satisfies the requirements placed on an ecological building material. Building with concrete meets the current and planned demands for reusability.

References:
[1] Report of behalf of the Bundesverband Baustoffe, Steine & Erden e.V.: Langfristige Entwicklung des Verbrauchs wichtiger Steine und Erden – Rohstoffe in der Bundesrepublik Deutschland, Berlin, 1999
[2] Federal Institute for Geosciences and Natural Resources: Flächenbedarf für den Abbau von oberflächennahen Rohstoffen im Jahr 1997; in: Commodity Top News 9/2000
[3] Report of behalf of the Bundesverband Baustoffe, Steine & Erden e.V.: Technische, ökologische und wirtschaftliche Einflüsse an der derzeitigen und zukünftigen Mengen an rezyklierten Baustoffen, Heidelberg, 1999
[4] Kreislaufwirtschaftsträger Bau: 3. Monitoring-Bericht Bauabfälle (Erhebung 2000), Berlin, 2003

Designing with concrete

Building with precast concrete elements – design options

Andreas Hild
Dionys Ottl

In today's "production" of architecture, what was once the manual assembling of building materials is now often the combining of industrially prefabricated semi-finished goods. However, the term "prefabricated" can lead the planner astray. For precast (reinforced) concrete elements are not ready-to-use semi-finished goods, but rather factory-produced bespoke components for specific applications. In this sense they are less "prefabricated" than the majority of building products used these days. They are produced as individual elements for specific applications, and the architect really acts as a planner in their development.

Designing with precast concrete elements

It is frequently the case that the use of precast concrete elements is restricted to areas that are no longer visible once the structure is finished. In most cases they are structural elements prefabricated for economic reasons under pressure of time and costs. In principle, however, precast concrete elements are suitable for virtually any part of the structure. Their potential applications are numerous and diverse.
In practice we distinguish between frame and solid wall forms of construction, and there are also various hybrid forms. The jointing and connecting of precast concrete elements works in a similar way to a giant "building kit" and is subject to similar, simple rules, provided the "builders" adhere to certain principles.

One crucial difference between precast concrete and in situ concrete is its element-based form and therefore the limited number of formats, also the series-based and rational use of forms in which small batches of elements are cast. However, these precast concrete elements need not necessarily be identical; indeed, in many cases they are identical only at first sight. Structural engineering requirements prescribe differences for individual loading cases. Different positions in the structure and different reinforcements lead to only very few identical elements – if at all – on the building site, even if they all originate from the same mould. In contrast to industrialised system building, the individual elements these days really are individual in the majority of cases, produced for specific locations, i.e. visually identical small series with varying internal details.

Precast concrete elements offer several advantages over in situ concrete. Besides the opportunities for complicated formwork patterns and component geometries, the essential advantage of precast concrete lies in its factory-based production, which takes place under controlled conditions protected from the vagaries of the weather. Such factors are especially critical for the quality of surface finish, the concrete density, precise contours and high-quality colours. The limits placed on the sizes of individual elements and the ensuing need for butt joints are often seen as disadvantages. The sizes of the individual elements depend on the technical options of the precasting works, e.g. the formats of the casting beds available, and also transportation options. The risk of damage during transport and erection are also major factors which influence the basic design of elements.

Production and design
Precast concrete elements are fabricated in horizontal or vertical forms depending on the formats and the production options of the precasting works. The surface finishes of elements cast vertically hardly differ from those of in situ concrete. However, wall or column elements can also be cast horizontally on a casting

bed. Where it touches the formwork, the concrete of course mirrors the inside face of the formwork, but on the open side a manually trowelled or floated finish is customary. This results in two different surface finishes: the formwork side and the smooth (floated/trowelled) side. Besides the use of form liners, which leave an imprint in the concrete, it is also possible to treat the surface of the open side using various techniques. If the open surface is left untreated, the result after compacting (vibrating) the concrete is a very rough, irregular surface. However, the open surface is usually trowelled or floated to a certain degree, right up to the creation of a precise, flat surface by means of power floating. The options for working the surface and the choice of tools for doing so are limited only by the architect's imagination.

Coloured concrete is usually more successful with precast concrete than with in situ concrete because the quality of the concrete, the humidity of the air and the curing time can be better controlled in the works than on the building site. Nevertheless, even with precast elements, owing to the choice of aggregate, coloured concrete is still a difficult subject which requires detailed, careful planning and preparations. The production of coloured concrete calls for considerable experience and knowledge about concrete mixes and the effects of pigments in order to achieve a reproducible, constant product.

Further primary design features of precast concrete elements are the sizes and the joints. Whereas in situ concrete can imitate precast concrete through the inclusion of dummy joints, the opposite effect is not possible. The joints always reveal the presence of prefabricated elements. In the case of loadbearing ele-

ments, the structural requirements govern the form of the joints.

One special case is the semi-prefabricated element, which is in reality permanent formwork made from fair-face concrete to which in situ concrete is then added. Besides the standard use in the form of small-format flooring units which help to speed up progress on site, such elements are also used when the appearance of precast concrete is desired but in situ concrete systems must be used for structural purposes.

All the aspects mentioned in the foregoing result in a wide range of possibilities, especially if these aspects are considered in varying combinations. Building with precast concrete elements therefore requires a sound knowledge of the various techniques and requirements, which presumes close cooperation between structural engineer, contractor and architect.

1a–c Erection of precast concrete facade elements, multi-storey car park, Munich, 2002; architects: Hild & K Architekten

Multi-storey car park, Munich

1

Riem is a suburb of Munich and the home of Munich's trade fair grounds. The parking concept included a multi-storey car park with 600 spaces in which local residents could also rent spaces. The developer was also the contractor, who also owned a precasting works specialising in systems for multi-storey car parks. Hild & K Architekten was appointed to design the facade. In accordance with the Bavarian Building Code, the facade had to have openings for ventilation amounting to approx. 30% of the total area. The building is situated in an urban setting among other buildings. In order to guarantee the necessary sound insulation the south side had to have an essentially closed facade, which meant that the ventilation openings had to be distributed over the remaining facade areas.

The building is designed as a reinforced concrete frame in a system building form of construction with loadbearing external walls at both ends. The internal structure consists of in situ concrete columns with column heads and supporting flat slabs. Precast elements are used for the loadbearing walls. The precast elements were cast vertically in the battery forms of a semi-automatic, hydraulic casting plant. The sizes of such individual elements depend on the production options of the battery forms and the transportation.

The wall elements were erected storey by storey and connected to the in situ concrete floors, which are visible externally as narrow grey bands. The design brief called for sharp edges. In practice these were difficult to realise because there were elements in the corners of all storeys at the junctions with the end walls where the loads were such that the elements could not be precast, but instead had to be cast in situ.

The structural concept of the building affects the facades considerably. Therefore, the notion of treating the surface of a precast concrete facade in isolation soon proved to be unsatisfactory. The architects quickly abandoned the idea of placing plastic liners in the forms because of the high cost of fabrication and maintenance, and because the abundance of ready-made liners for a variety of concrete structures results in a certain arbitrariness. The architects wanted not only to determine the external surface of the building, but to use the facade to help determine the interior as well. They achieved this by shaping the top and bottom edges of the precast spandrel panels.

The facade elements were cast horizontally in steel forms which are normally used for precasting bridge beams. This meant that the length of the individual parts in this case was determined not by the size of the casting bed, but solely by the transport options. The vehicles, cranes, etc. available restricted the length of the elements to a relatively generous size of 14 m. The interim storage of the elements with their precise edges – left unprotected to reduce the costs – caused considerable difficulties, as did their transportation which had to be vertically on their "wavy" edges.

2

3

4

In order to give the impression of a freely designed form, the spandrel panels were cast in two mirror-image forms and erected in "mirrored" or "rotated" variations. The combination of the various possibilities plus the offsetting of joints allowed the series production of the parts to recede into the background and enabled the creation of constantly changing contours.
In order to enhance the contrast between the freely designed facade form and the background, iron ferrite was added at the works to give the precast wall elements a darker colouring. The "wavy" spandrel panels, on the other hand, are made from an almost white concrete, which forms the basis for concrete of any colour – even black. Grey cement for the in situ concrete components makes up the trio of external colours. The internal components were given a yellow glaze after completion, a technique that allows the irregularities and the texture of the concrete to shine through but nevertheless provides colour.

Multi-storey car park, Munich, 2002
Architects: Hild & K Architekten, Munich
Structural engineers: Haumann & Fuchs, Traunstein

1 View from east
2 Location plan, scale 1:2000
  a car park
  b Building Centre
3 Forms for "wavy" spandrel panels
4 Erection of Z-shaped wall element
5 Vertical section through "wavy" spandrel panel, scale 1:20
  a flat slab, reinforced concrete, 300 mm
  b precast concrete panel, 150 mm
  c cast-in steel channel, 140 mm
  d column
  e safety barrier: steel reinforcing mesh, painted black
6 Interior view of car park

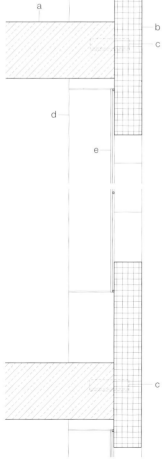

5

6

Building Centre, Munich

1

Munich's Building Centre is a sort of permanent trade fair for building products. Situated close to the trade fair grounds, it is designed to become established as an extension to the building fair and provide a point of contact for the building industry all year round. An exhibition covering methods of building and special components, especially interior fitting-out, is aimed at private developers. In addition, seminars and events dealing with many construction topics are held here. Like its neighbour, the multi-storey car park described on pp. 52–53, the developer was also the contractor. The long-term plan is that the structure will be made available to the City of Munich in a sort of public-private partnership arrangement. The framework conditions called for a low-cost, fast-build project. The concept was therefore to present the fitting-out products of the exhibitors against the backdrop of an untreated, exposed structure. The whole of the north side of the building was conceived as rows of large display windows; the generous expanse of glazing provides views into the building, but also views out, over trade fair events. A multi-flight single staircase behind the facade links the various exhibition floors.

Design
The Building Centre is designed as a monolithic construction, without intermediate columns, based on three-layer concrete sandwich elements: core insulation is applied to a loadbearing concrete leaf and covered with a thinner concrete facing leaf. This creates a homogeneous multi-layer element that can be erected as a finished wall element without any further treatment.
However, this apparently simple design proved to be a complex component in practice. Even fixing the facing leaf through the insulation to the loadbearing leaf requires careful detailing to avoid

thermal bridges. Furthermore, the design of the butt joints and, in particular, their airtightness and watertightness had to be considered. Normally, the facing leaf – a homogeneous component – is used as the outer, visible side in order to overcome building performance problems. It is also used at the junctions between loadbearing components, although a reversal in the sequence of layers is conceivable.

Two component types were developed for this building. Uninsulated elements from series production using battery forms were used for the area adjacent to the neighbouring multi-storey car park. Here, the grouted joints between the individual elements were left very wide in order to provide space for building services. In many precast concrete buildings these are simply surface-mounted, or cast in at the precasting works – at considerable expense.
Contrasting with this, the sandwich elements described above were used on the facade with the windows and on the end walls. Owing to the large window openings, these elements, measuring about 7 x 3.5 m, lack rigidity and were correspondingly difficult to transport and erect. Traditional metal window frames were not used. Instead, the windows are seated on stainless steel studs that protrude directly from the precast concrete element, and are held in place by concrete "beads" in a contrasting colour. Considering the tolerances and deformations common in such buildings, this is a very demanding form of construction. However, compared to conventional post-and-rail solutions, it still proved to be very cost-effective, at least for this project. The multi-layer sandwich panels were cast with the external wall element (with dense fair-face concrete side) on the underside, the internal wall element on top. The latter was

finished manually after casting with a lamb's wool roller.

The building rigorously avoids any form of fitting-out. There is neither a screed nor any impact sound insulation. The power-floated, colourless-impregnated concrete slab is at the same time the wearing course. Walls and soffits were also left untreated. In a sense, the building is a sort of refined, compacted raw carcass in which fitting-out components are shown only within the exhibition itself.

4, 5 Sections through window, scale 1:20
  a precast concrete parapet element, 200 mm
  b wall construction: precast concrete element consisting of 120 mm reinforced concrete facing leaf (Kiefersfeldener cement with 3% black pigment), 120 mm rigid thermal insulation, 240 mm reinforced concrete loadbearing leaf (Kiefersfeldener cement with 3% black pigment), precast concrete elements grouted internally, with 240 mm in situ concrete strips
  c precast concrete glazing "bead" (Burglengenfelder cement), 200 x 2100 mm
  d glazing: 8 mm toughened safety glass + 16 mm cavity + 16 mm laminated safety glass in reinforced concrete frame, size of pane: 2360 x 2310 mm
  e glass support: stainless steel radial rocker bearing in cube
  f seal, black

Building Centre, Munich, 2004
Architects: Hild & K Architekten, Munich
Structural engineers: Haumann & Fuchs, Traunstein

1 View from north
2 Erection of precast concrete window frames
3 Erection of glass
6 Exhibition area

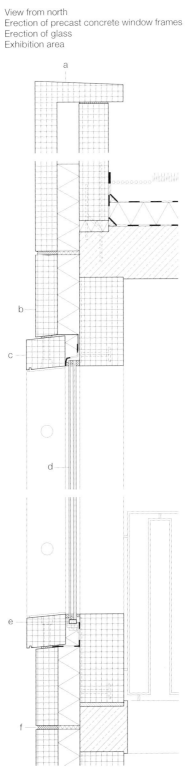

Laboratory building, Munich

B.F.T.S. Research Institute, Munich, 2004
Architects: Hild & K Architekten, Munich
1   Location plan, scale 1:4000
2   Corridor on ground floor
4   View from north
3, 5 Sections, scale 1:20
    a wall construction:
      glaze finish
      120 mm thermal insulation composite system,
      bonded
      250 mm precast fair-face concrete elemen
    b cable duct
    c metal window with double glazing
    d floor construction:
      16 mm sports floor
      64 mm reinforced screed
      PE sheeting as separating layer
      2 No. 20 mm impact sound insulation
      200 mm reinforced concrete

The Bavarian Research and Technology Centre for Sports Studies is an institute with laboratories, diagnostics rooms and studios plus various offices and seminar zones. As part of the " Bavarian Future Offensive" project with its demanding layout and technical fitting-out profile, the building was only approved on the basis of extreme funding cutbacks well below the cost parameters. Multi-tiered reductions in funding complicated the planning work again and again. The developer wanted a closely spaced grid to achieve the desired layout, which under these conditions was not feasible in the form of a frame with curtain wall facade. In order to achieve a fast, cost-effective solution, a concrete building with an insulating render facade was chosen instead, following comparative analyses of the costs. This form of construction even works as a low-energy house – a side-effect that has no effect on the costs. During cost cutting exercise, almost the entire interior fitting-out was gradually reduced to a flexible dry wall solution within a monolithic carcass.

The developer's approach was to complete all the design work (including details) prior to inviting tenders and appointing contractors, which considerably restricted the opportunities to react to variations brought about by the construction and the contractors' bids. Originally conceived as a pure in situ concrete structure, pressing deadlines forced the main parts of the building to be redesigned in precast concrete during the planning and tendering stages. Only the two end sections were left as in situ concrete structures to provide stability. The entire middle section (only the external walls of which are solid construction to leave a flexible interior) was conceived as a precast concrete envelope with loadbearing external walls. Instead of the in situ con-

crete walls which had originally beenenvisaged positioned between the windows, the loadbearing structure had to be changed to a plate-like, small-format wall construction with storey-high individual elements on a 2.40 m grid. A jointless facade was required in order to minimise the weaknesses of a thermal insulation composite system, but this proved particularly difficult to realise. The concept also called for calculation of dimensions and precise jointing of the elements in order to guarantee no long-term movements of the structural shell after completion.
The individual parts of the building were

built in phases. After completing the two end sections in separate concreting operations, the external wall elements were erected, even though each of the next storeys of the end sections had to be completed before building the middle section in order to be able to erect the intermediate floors safely between the external walls. Positioning of the building services was eased through pairs of columns placed off-centre, between which the vertical service runs and flat floor slabs were positioned for a flexible horizontal layout. Whereas the precast concrete elements presented no problems for the

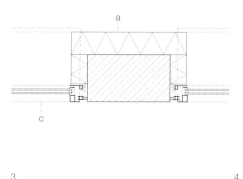

3

4

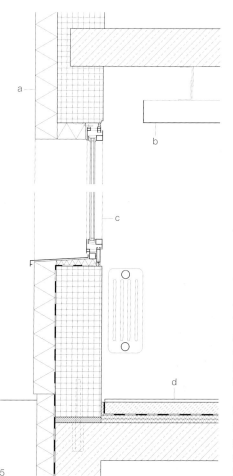

5

contractor, the production of fair-face concrete surfaces on site posed some obstacles. The contractor, who had been appointed following a public-sector tendering procedure, felt unable to comply with the specification for the end sections despite their simple form of construction. Therefore, the entire interior layout, which up to this time had been based on fair-face concrete surfaces, had to be adapted to meet this new situation without causing additional cost.

As the facade components were of a high quality, it was possible to implement the idea of an exposed structure as a counterweight to the fully insulated external skin. However, the resulting, small-format pattern of joints had to be rearranged. Instead of the visible imprint of the formwork for the in situ concrete, matching the building grid exactly, the layout had to be more generous, but still remain within the scope of the limited construction options.

In the end, all the components – with the exception of the junctions with the end sections – were based on an identical concept. The butt joints were positioned in the sides of the narrow window reveals and continued around these as a continuous line. Instead of two construction joints, however, this form of construction led to a number of "expansion joints", with the risk that these could become visible in the sensitive thermal insulation facade despite the movement calculations for the building being based on no joints. Furthermore, by transferring the rough, vibrated side of the precast concrete element to the outside, a considerable variation in surface tolerances had to be accepted, which the contractor could not minimise despite precise alignment. Items cast into the facade therefore had to be adapted accordingly. This variation in tolerances in two directions (vertically and horizontally) was especially problematic for the rigid thermal insulation system because of increased risk of cracking in the external skin.
The flush fitting of the windows, considerably important for the uniform grid of the entire building, had already been established when erecting the loadbearing structure.

In contrast to traditional masonry construction, which through the building of a homogeneous, loadbearing and insulating layer can reliably accommodate deviations in tolerances, the degree of precision required for the design and construction of the insulated external skin in concrete components is considerably higher. Deviations and fluctuations in tolerances cannot easily be compensated for and accumulate very rapidly. This can lead to considerable reductions in the thickness of the insulating material, which causes building performance problems.

Besides the insulation, components relevant to the facade such as sunshades, cable ducts or fixings have to be planned in detail at an early stage in order to check the effects on the design or building of the facade, and to finalise the positions of openings, cast-in items and unavoidable changes in level. Contrary to the opinions of some manufacturers that attaching full thermal insulation to a structure is a visual substitute for a rendered facade, this approach significantly alters a structure and calls for – besides strict workmanship rules for junctions and surfaces – an individual design strategy in order to create an effect appropriate to this form of construction.

Concrete projects

Martin Peck

Defining responsibilities

It is not possible to discuss the organisation of contractual responsibility for the compilation and award of design and building contracts for all the world's different legal systems. Nevertheless, in the light of experience gained from everyday practical building activities on large concrete projects in Germany, Europe and elsewhere, it is certainly necessary to investigate the significance of and boundaries between the contractual responsibilities of the different professional groups and partners involved. The natural boundary between the responsibilities for the design and construction of a structure are explained by the traditional division of work between the architect designing the structure and the building contractor working to the architect's drawings. Despite differences in national legal systems, this boundary is recognisable in almost all countries of the world and in most cases is reflected in standards and civil law. The options for organising design or building contracts for carrying out construction activities vary enormously even in Western legal systems, with, in some cases, very different national characteristics and customs. The variations are evident in the individual national spheres of influence and are an effect of globalisation. Owing to the international business activities of large design offices and building contractors, contractual models from other legal systems have been absorbed into the respective national systems, provided their conditions are compatible with the respective legal system and are advantageous for at least one of the parties to the contract. The traditional Western contract model is the measurement contract in which the designer plans and specifies every trade and every activity as an item in a schedule (bill of quantities). This type of planning and the awarding of contracts for building works requires a very detailed interaction between the activities of the designer and those of the contractor – more than any other form of contract. It creates countless transitions and interfaces, transfers of responsibility and grey areas which have to be overcome in everyday practical building operations and frequently lead to a series of characteristic problems. It is therefore important and sensible to look first at the fundamental definitions of responsibilities for design and construction, especially in light of the popularity of the measurement contract model. The following information is based largely on data obtained from Germany and other member states of the European Union.

The reconfiguration of the codes of practice for concrete buildings in the member states of the European Union is in structural terms based on the conventional division of work and responsibility among the professional groups and market partners involved in the design and construction of a structure.

In terms of designing a concrete structure, it is essential to discuss first just

1   PHAENO Science Centre, Wolfsburg, Germany,
    2005; architect: Zaha Hadid, with Mayer/Bährle   1

what and how much the designer should, must or may design. This discussion tackles the often difficult task of the designer, who has to describe his design work adequately and completely but without restricting the contractor's choice of materials and methods – or innovativeness. The current legal framework and the structure of the codes of practice place the designer at a distinct distance from the building operations themselves. In order to understand the boundary between design and construction responsibilities in each case, it is helpful to consider design and construction as a "target–path system". The designer should aim to formulate solely the building contract targets using the generally acknowledged terminology and concepts of the technical codes of practice. The task of the builder is then to select technically suitable and economic paths from the multitude of technical possibilities for realising the targets of the designer, within the applicable framework conditions. The freedom of choice with respect to the path gives the builder the chance to steer the technical and economic success of his approach based on his own capacities and abilities, and supplies motivation for independent action.

If target and path are already confused at the design stage and in the subsequent building contract, it is usually difficult to overcome such lack of focus during everyday practical building and site management activities. Here is a practical example:

Situation

For the production of surfaces with a high-quality fair-face concrete finish, the designer describes the properties of the surfaces with adequate accuracy in the tender and adds an item to his bill of quantities (BOQ) which calls for the production of trial panels. The trial panels shall be used to specify the final surface quality together with the contractor. Drawing on experience from previous projects, the designer adds a "technical specification" to the conditions of contract which contains obligatory information and restrictions regarding the materials to be used to produce fair-face concrete surfaces. The following is an extract from the conditions of contract:

Extract from contract:
X. Additional technical conditions of contract
X.1 Fair-face concrete, BOQ items M.MMM to N.NNN
X.1.1 Technical specification for materials to be used
X.1.1.1 Formwork
The formwork panels for producing fair-face concrete surfaces must be smooth, without any texture and non-absorbent, and the surface of the formwork panels must be finished with a waterproof polyphenolic coating.

Remarks:
Specifying a waterproof polyphenolic coating restricts the numerous technical options for producing a smooth, non-absorbent formwork surface to just one group of products. This is not advisable when trying to achieve a high-quality surface finish because it means the contractual exclusion of better-quality new developments.

X.1.1.2 Concrete
Only Portland cement type CEM I 32.5 may be used for producing the concrete. The minimum cement content in the concrete shall be 320 kg/m³. The sand/cement content of the concrete shall be adequate for the production of fair-face concrete. The effective water/cement ratio of the concrete should be max. 0.55. At the time of placement the maximum dimension of the concrete in the flow table test shall be 450 mm.

Remarks:
This contract provision certainly contains details relevant to building operations. It describes one possible path that can be taken to achieve a high-quality fair-face concrete surface. However, the planning of building operations and hence also the selection of the concrete mix and other raw materials should remain the obligation and choice of the contractor. He is contractually responsible for the quality of the finished surfaces and should not be hampered by placing restrictions on his building operations. In addition, specifying a minimum cement content, a maximum water/cement ratio and a maximum flow table test dimension is excessive because these parameters are interrelated. Such a specification usually makes it impossible to produce a suitable concrete and achieve the required surface quality. Conditions of contract regarding concrete mixes frequently have to be retracted after the first practical trials.

2

The contractual provisions given above are typical of many everyday building contracts concerning fair-face concrete. We can see the intention of the designer, who tries to specify the path to the target contractually, based on his own experience. However, as such provisions cause the designer to encroach on the contractor's sphere of responsibility, the former is contractually responsible if the procedures he has specified do not lead to the desired success. In the example given above the designer is responsible, for example, for the concrete mix because it has been specified in the contract documents. This restricts the contractor's freedom needlessly and causes him unnecessary difficulties and costs if the concrete mix specified proves to be unsuitable and trials are required to find the appropriate mix.

In the above case the knowledge and experience of the contractor is constricted by specifying the formwork panel and concrete mix in the contract documents. However, as the contractor is in the end contractually responsible for the overall success ("high-quality fair-face concrete surfaces"), the realisation of his innovative abilities can be achieved only via a time-consuming and costly alternative path. The contractual stipulations must be checked for feasibility in practical trials and, if necessary, changes have to be negotiated.

It is not always easy to keep target and path separate in everyday design activities because the defining criteria are often imprecise. One example of the right "boundary feeling" is revealed by a taxi journey in an unknown city:
The taxi passenger (designer) climbs into a taxi and states his destination (contractual provisions and properties of building components). The taxi driver has local knowledge (abilities, codes of practice) and a suitable vehicle (personnel and plant) in order to transport the passenger safely to his desired destination. No sensible taxi passenger would tell the taxi driver to drive on just three wheels or use third gear only, and in a strange city would also not dream of navigating himself!

Contractual relationship
It is difficult to specify a generally applicable sequence for the pre-contract planning of building measures because every construction project represents an individual case which may call for deviations

from customary procedures. Projects for public-sector clients are frequently prescribed by fixed administrative documents (in Germany this is the VOB: Contract Procedures for Building Works). In private-sector projects the designer usually has the task, and the freedom, to specify the rules according to which the design, award of contract and construction should proceed, or at least shape them a large extent. This results in duties and opportunities for the designer.

The client generally awards two different types of contract for the design and construction of a building:

· The design and site management are usually awarded, performed and reimbursed on the basis of engineering contracts, possibly founded on appropriate scales of fees (in Germany the HOAI: Official Scale of Fees for Services by Architects and Engineers). The client's contractual partner is in most cases the architect, who will appoint specialists to carry out certain design activities (e.g. structural engineering) in the course of the overall planning of the project.

· The construction work is awarded to a qualified building contractor, which leads to a building contract being drawn up. The legal basis of every contract is the applicable civil law (in Germany the BGB: German Civil Code), defined more precisely, if necessary, by adding specific business terms and conditions, provided these are compatible with the relevant legal system (Germany: VOB). The building contract describes the contractual performance in terms of type and quantity plus the time in which the work is to be carried out. It forms the foundation for assessing the contractual performance and regulates acceptance and reimbursement, payment conditions and warranties.

The preparation of the building contract and its technical formulation are generally in the designer's remit. The client adds economic framework conditions, e.g. terms of payment, safety/security aspects or warranty details, to the technical content of the contract. It should be ensured that the pricing information of the tenderer is completed when the tender is submitted and hence prior to the final conclusion of the contract between client and contractor. The subsequent addition of work or contractual conditions that were not considered in the tenderer's calculations and represent a technical or economic difficulty for the tenderer require renegotiation of the total price taking into account the additional work.

There is not usually any contractual relationship between the designer responsible for site management and the contractor carrying out the building work. However, in the interests of successful site management, it is essential for the designer to have some authority to issue instructions to the contractor. It must be possible for the designer to reject or stop in good time defective works or those not in accordance with the contract, also in the sense of limiting the damage for all those involved. The designer must be able to accept without undue delay parts of the work that will be concealed by subsequent measures, or to demand rectification of inadequate work. However, the designer is usually not authorised – neither by the building contract nor his own design contract – to issue instructions to the contractor.

This fact normally has no effect in practice because the contractor requires the collaboration of the designer and will usu-ally follow his instructions without checking the contractual background. Nevertheless, there is some uncertainty as to the legal situation, which can result in unpleasant consequences for all those involved, especially in serious disputes and when the designer's decisions have financial repercussions. The client should therefore assign to the designer some of his contractual rights with respect to the contractor in the form of a proxy. Just what the site management may decide and in which cases information from or the agreement of the client is required must be unambiguous for site management and contractor at all times.

Concrete – from design to ordering

Design details (provided by structural engineer)

Volume of concrete	4.5 m³
Ambient conditions	weather, frost, no de-icing salts
Exposure classes	XC4, XF1
Compressive strength class required for structural purposes	C16/20
Minimum compressive strength class (XC4, XF1)	C25/30
Fair-face concrete requirements	none
Other requirements	none
Component geometry and reinforcement content	to working drawing item XX.xxx

Bill of quantities item (designer)

Item: XX.xxx

Quantity	Units	Description	Unit price [€/m³]	Total price [€]
4.5	m³	Concrete to DIN EN 206-1/DIN EN 1045-2, exposure classes XC4, XF1, compressive strength class C 25/30, cast, compacted and cured in formwork to working drawing XX.xxx to DIN EN 1045-3		

Specification data for concrete (design data and on-site properties)

Details from designer (bill of quantities, drawing)	exposure classes XC4, XF1 compressive strength class C 25/30
Building operations (selected by contractor)	consistence class F3 max. aggregate size 16 mm moderate strength development

Concrete as ordered by the contractor

Ready-mixed concrete	Concrete to DIN EN 206-1/DIN EN 1045-2; XC4, XF1; C 25/30; F3; 16 mm; moderate strength development

4

2 Erection of a building with complex geometry using in situ concrete, Mercedes-Benz Museum, Stuttgart, Germany, 2006; architects: UN studio, van Berkel & Bos
3 Description of the technical properties of concrete from planning to production

Bill of quantities (BOQ)

While preparing the building contract, the designer first compiles the tender documents. In standard measurement contracts a key element of the tender and the subsequent building contract is the specification. This consists of the bill of quantities at least, in which the contractual performance – subdivided into sensible activities – is listed in detail and separately according to building components and stages of the work. If applicable, the specification also includes conditions for the construction wherever these cause costs directly or indirectly. The bill of quantities is compiled using the quantities calculated beforehand, i.e. the numbers, sizes, areas, lengths or volumes of the individual components and the work required to provide them. The bill of quantities is therefore a schedule of parts of the work, listed and numbered in a comprehensible arrangement. Every item contains the following information:

- *Details of location* (also drawings, design documents, etc.) from which it is clear where, i.e. in which component or part of a component, the work is to be carried out. It is helpful to supplement the bill of quantities with technical documents and to provide clear cross-references to these. The location of the work is mostly evident from the numbering system of the bill of quantities.
- *Details of quantities*, which indicates the scope of the work to be carried out. This information can be in the form of a number, size, area, length or volume and is estimated based on the status of the design at the time of compiling the tender. The tenderer, i.e. the building contractor, who estimates the work required and offers a tender initially supplies a unit price for every part of the work which relates to the unit of measurement of the quantities, and in a second step multiplies the price by the unit of measurement to obtain a total price for that item of the work.
- A *descriptive text* in which the work is specified in more detail. The descriptive text should be formulated concisely and unambiguously using the customary terminology and designations. Every part of the work can include incidental works in addition to the principal works. If the part of the work is to include incidental works, it is helpful to refer to these in the text (e.g. transport to/from site, setting up, maintenance, dismantling and disposal).

The term "incidental works" describes works that are so closely related to the principal works (in the sense of technical building operations) that they must be added to the price of this work and are not to be listed separately. Payment for incidental works is included in that for the principal works.

What this means for the designer compiling the tender is that incidental works do not have to be listed separately, and they are reimbursed together with the principal works. The tenderer must include the cost of incident works in the unit price for the principal works.

5   Fixing steel mesh reinforcement with the help of a crane, Lufthansa head office, Frankfurt/Main, Germany, 2005; architects: Ingenhoven & Partner, Düsseldorf

The corresponding legal frameworks recognise examples of typical incidental works, but there is nevertheless no generally applicable, adequate description for incidental works. The definition of incidental works is therefore difficult in each case and again and again leads to disputes about payment for works that the designer understands as incidental works but the contractor as separate works which must be reimbursed separately. It is therefore advisable to describe incidental works in the descriptive texts where possible or to include them as separate items in a bill of quantities when they exceed a certain value.

The bill of quantities is the key document on which every tenderer bases his price and must satisfy certain requirements:

- Every part of the work must be described in detail, clearly and comprehensively for every tenderer. In other words, every tenderer must be able to discern the same work from the description and from this be able to calculate a price without undue effort (Germany: VOB part A, cl. 9 "Description of works").
- The total of the parts of the work should describe the overall works fully and without omissions. In other words, nothing should be absent from the description of the works and there should be no significant contradictions with regard to quantities.

The applicable legislation regarding measurement contracts (Germany: VOB part A) calls for a simple, uncomplicated and generally understandable description of the works in a building contract with specification (measurement contract). The designer should also adhere to this requirement even if he is not bound by such legislation during design work and preparation of the contract documents because, generally speaking, the legal fraternity will essentially decide according to such criteria if called upon to assess a specification. Works that are not listed in the bill of quantities and do not represent incidental works but are necessary for fulfilling the contract may entitle the contractor to submit a claim. This applies when the quantity given for an item in the bill of quantities is considerably exceeded, e.g. by more than 10%, when actually carrying out work. It is important to ensure that quantities estimated in the course of the design work are in principle of only limited accuracy. However, deviations of 10% and more are rare when designing new building works.

The local circumstances and conditions relevant to the building works must be assessed in detail prior to compiling the bill of quantities. Such assessments often reveal noise, dust, waste-water and site logistics restrictions which may force expensive solutions when selecting methods of construction. Elaborate, costly protection and circulation measures for the public may be required in the case of neighbouring residential or commercial buildings. Environmental stipulations or the functions of adjoining buildings (sheltered housing, hospitals, etc.) may call for special measures to limit noise, or may place restrictions on the working hours of the building site. The designer should be aware of this when estimating the costs, or at least, when compiling the bill of quantities.

The aspects outlined above should be clarified and agreed by the designer in consultation with the client. They are essential for the costs indemnity, for the quality of the design and for ensuring trouble-free building operations completed on time. If such aspects lead to contractual restrictions, it is not usually possible to consider these in the items of the bill of quantities; instead, they must be regulated in other contract documents.

The building contract
The many building contract models available for new building works hardly have an influence on the actual design and construction, but rather vary only in terms of the contractual responsibilities. The building contract customarily used in Germany is the VOB measurement contract, which is based on the traditional division of responsibilities between design and construction.

In the case of public-sector clients, invitations to tender are generally open (publicly advertised) and do not impose any restrictions on who may submit a tender. The award of a contract follows clear guidelines in order to guarantee equal opportunities among the tenderers and rule out any influences caused by the interests of individuals. For this very reason, German legislation, for example, contains comprehensive and detailed rules about tendering procedures, checking and evaluation of tenders and awarding of contracts for public-sector building contracts (VOB part A). Where such legislation or statutory instruments dealing with tenders for building contracts exist, it is primarily the rules regarding awarding of contracts that are especially interesting because these – depending on market relationships – are directly significant prerequisites for quality construction.

Rules on the awarding of contracts are normally formulated with the intention of appointing a tenderer who can provide quality building works for the most cost-effective price while exploiting the laws of the open market.

However, in practice problems arise precisely due to such stipulations and the way in which they are applied. The assessment of the tenders will include checking the suitability of the tenderer, the content of the work on offer and the adequacy of the price. A positive assessment of the tenderer and the correctness of the content are essential prerequisites for awarding a contract. However, it is almost always the price that is critical.

A low price is a very clear – and for the client always an attractive – criterion on which to base the award of a contract. On the other hand, the assessment of a tender can prove difficult in individual cases and the outcome depends on certain points, or on the tenderer's readiness to collaborate. Added to this is the fact that the poor suitability of a tenderer or the inadequacy of a price can sometimes be difficult to validate.

The rejection of a tender based on such criteria is often difficult to uphold if the tenderer makes a formal complaint. In addition, a complaint may delay the award of the contract and put the project timetable in jeopardy.

The designer involved in the planning (and later the site management) of a construction project for a public-sector client usually has little or no influence on the outcome of the procedure in the case of an open tendering process. The recognition in a public-sector construction project that it is easier to be awarded a contract through a low-budget price than through sound calculation to achieve quality construction in the end also has a significance for the economic and technical success of the designer with site management duties.

In the case of private-sector projects, the organisational procedures during design and the awarding of the contract are usually left to the discretion of the designer, or are determined in consultation with the client. In some cases this can offer advantages, particularly in terms of the unrestricted definition of the criteria for awarding contracts. However, it is always advisable to organise the building contract strictly in accordance with the national building regulations and all applicable legal conditions because the use of customary contractual terminology, formulations and procedures guarantees better technical and legal indemnity.

Advice on implementation

Depending on the architectural or engineering complexity, the production of concrete and reinforced concrete components may prove to be very demanding from a technical point of view. The success of any concreting measures depends on the knowledge of the designer and the skills and manpower capacities of the contractor. In his own interests as well, the designer should obtain information – preferably before awarding the contract – about the capabilities of the individual tenderers. This is especially relevant for building measures for private-sector clients in which the designer generally has a greater say in awarding the contract (in conjunction with the client). It is preferable in many cases to limit the number of tenderers right from the start of the tendering and award of contract process, for the following reasons:

- It reduces the work of processing the tenders.
- Selecting a group of tenderers according to the experience of the designer and client can have a positive influence on the quality of the building works.
- The number of unsuccessful tenderers in the process is also limited, each tenderer's chance of being awarded the contract is relatively high.

If selective tendering is employed, a limited number of chosen contractors are sent the tender documents and invited to submit a price. This approach presumes that the designer and/or the client knows a significant number of potential contractors with appropriate qualifications and is in a position to reach a sensible decision. Generally, it is preferable to invite at least three, but never more than 10, potential contractors to tender for the work. In addition, a regional radius should be adhered to when selecting candidates. The radius should correspond to the economic scope of the building measures and be chosen such that every tenderer can visit the location of the site at reasonable cost. If the planned construction project is particularly large or involves special difficulties due to local conditions, a site visit for each tenderer should be made compulsory. But in the selective tendering procedure as well, the final criterion on which the decision to award the contract to a certain tenderer is the competitiveness of the price: in other words, the "cheapest" price after checking and comparing the contents of the tenders.

Yet another method is recommended when awarding contracts for especially large or difficult construction projects. An "eligibility competition", i.e. prequalification, (see VOB part A, cl. 3, para. 3, 2) is only advisable for particularly complex or large projects or when the designer feels that a tenderer with special qualifications is required to carry out the work and such abilities cannot be reliably assessed using the standard criteria. In cases where knowledge of the market shows that only a very limited group of contractors is in a position to carry out the work and choosing tenderers for selective tendering is inadvisable, potential tenderers can be selected in a prequalification round. In the prequalification round (usually an open process), the tenderers present their proposals, potential solutions and alternatives and the respective costs thereof to the client, based on the key framework conditions of the planned project. After assessing the proposals, the contract is either awarded directly to the tenderer with the best technical and economic solution, or a shortlist of tenderers is invited to resubmit their tenders based on more detailed technical and economic information. The "winner" of this second round is awarded the contract. The main difference between this and open tendering is that a considerable portion of the design work is carried out by the tenderers right from the start and they qualify themselves primarily through the technical suitability and economic appeal of the solutions and methods chosen. Irrespective of the method of awarding the contract, it is recommended to hand over the tender documents to potential tenderers in a meeting, especially in the case of particularly difficult construction projects or those with high quality demands (e.g. fair-face concrete). Such meetings offer ideal opportunities for gaining an impression of the competence of each tenderer and for discussing certain requirements in detail. It is worthwhile recording the details discussed and the contractual requirements in writing. Checking the suitability of a tenderer should in any case involve other criteria apart from just the competitiveness of the price. Looking beyond the list of projects

carried out by the contractor is worthwhile because such lists do not necessarily include a sufficiently meaningful selection of projects completed.

Selective tendering and prequalification are solutions that can help to ensure that concreting works are awarded to capable and quality-oriented tenderers. However, the cooperation of the client in the award of contracts is mostly motivated by economic reasons. The awareness that high-quality construction must be rewarded adequately is sometimes difficult to uphold during the negotiations. The designer is not contractually bound to take part in the award of the contract and therefore can usually exert little influence on the financial negotiations between client and contractor, especially in the light of the ever decreasing flexibility in terms of money and hence quality. The building contract should therefore embody a reasonable price–performance configuration right from the start in order to guarantee a well-balanced contract even after negotiations. This is particularly important for the designer when he is also involved in site management.

Quality and site management

The design, tendering and award of contract duties are often followed by site management tasks. For the designer, site management of the project, i.e. representing the technical (and economic) interests of the client during construction, is usually the more important part of the design contract in economic terms. Management of the building site entails collaboration with the contractor, mostly according to the personnel- and operations-related working methods of the organisational systems and persons involved and also the works and processes in progress or waiting to begin. Coordination and communication, management and control of building operations by the designer in his site management role are rarities and they are usually only covered vaguely in the conditions of contract. However, the configuration of the building contract gives the designer a series of options for controlling and safeguarding the management of the building site and the ensuing quality through contractual provisions and routines without infringing on the sphere of responsibility of the contractor in the sense of the target–path separation. This can also regulate and ease the work of managing the building site considerably. Managing the building site and safeguarding the quality of construction go hand in hand; the means and measures to achieve these targets are essentially identical.

However, it must be made known to the contractor at the time of calculating his prices how the contract provisions regarding site management will affect his on-site operations. The work involved in, and cost of, such measures must be identifiable and calculable from the tender documents. This might mean, for example, that the contractor has to calculate his site personnel based on the stipulations and requirements of the building contract instead of his own operational customs and with a view to ensuring the optimum cost-effective approach.

Quality of workmanship

The quality of workmanship, assuming proper design, is directly dependent on the persons carrying out the work, i.e. the technical personnel of the building contractor. Site personnel usually includes the site manager, supervisory staff and the individual manual workers (divided into "gangs"). The skills, experience and numbers of site operatives, their availability and deployment, are decisive for the outcome of the work. Another critical factor is the personal dedication of the supervisory staff responsible. Besides practical experience on site, there are also verified findings:

During the 1990s Germany's Federal Highway Research Institute (BASt) carried out a survey of structural engineering projects in progress to discover the quality of workmanship on reinforced and prestressed concrete structures. The results were published in a report in 1999. They correspond very well with the experience gained on national and international building products and still remain up to date without any reservations. The following findings are particularly interesting:

- The report notes that subletting parts of the work to subcontractors generally leads to a distinct loss in quality. Besides the usual difficulties in overcoming the ensuing interfaces and the transfer of responsibility, the report also mentions other problems. One of these is that after subcontracting the responsibility for quality, the main contractor reduces his supervisory presence on the building site. Another is that subcontracted works often proceed simultaneously with a number of other trades, which can give the subcontractor a feeling of reduced importance and lack of recog-

7 a   b

nition for his own work. Furthermore, the distribution of responsibility for quality is often ambiguous, and there is also considerable pressure on prices. All these circumstances result in the subcontractor quickly losing his motivation to produce quality work.

• The report reveals that the quality of manual work depends primarily on supervision. The personal commitment of each member of a gang is essentially determined by the gang foreman. If this person is qualified, experienced and dedicated, then the members of the gang are mostly correspondingly motivated. The report also verifies that irrespective of the nationality of the workers, good workmanship is always achieved when the gang is led by a suitably qualified person.

The findings of the report can be directly implemented in the wording of the contract:

• The subletting of activities to subcontractors should be contractually prohibited or should require the consent of the parties involved.
• The qualifications of supervisory workers and the technical site management plus their deployment during concreting works should be regulated because these are critical factors for the ensuing quality and for the designer's site manager being able to exert a practical influence.

Site management
The prerequisite for organised and orderly management of the building site from the point of view of a designer with site management tasks is structured communications with the contractor. To do this, there should be simple, unambiguous network of information, notification and approval routines for individual

stages of the work (erecting formwork, fixing reinforcement, concreting, striking, curing) on different components or phases of the project.

The sequence of building operations for the stages of the work on the building site is determined by the contractor according to the respective on-site requirements. The designer's project manager can therefore only have sufficient information about current and planned operations when the contractor informs him comprehensively and in good time. In order to guarantee an adequate flow of information at all times, the contractor should be contractually obliged to set up a routine. The intensity of the flow of information can be adjusted to suit the respective circumstances.

In order that the designer can be informed in good time about preparations for important phases of the work, he should specify a practical length of time between receiving the information and the planned start of the respective activity.
Furthermore, it is advantageous when continuation of operations at quality-critical transitions between two phases of the work are linked to a formal approval prior to continuation or the acceptance of the actual condition. The designer in his site management role can decide in each case whether or not he wishes to inspect the actual condition prior to approving continuation of the work. The inspection option promotes an awareness of quality (for their own work) among the contractor's personnel.
However, contractual information routines based on notification and approval are only sensible and practical when limited to quality-critical works in the production of concrete components, and should be as straightforward as possible. Communication of critical facts in such routines should generally be in writing. As the

communication paths selected for the information and approval routines for building operations are also suitable for checking the deployment of the contractor's technical personnel by means of supervision and availability plans, this combines the aims of quality control and site management.

Summary of the measures
The measures that can be employed to manage the building site and safeguard the quality of workmanship can be incorporated in the contract as follows:

• Restricting the subletting of activities to subcontractors.
• Qualifications and number of personnel for technical site supervision.
• Qualifications, experience and number of supervisory personnel in every gang.
• Number and skills of personnel in formwork, steel-fixing and concreting gangs.
• Presence of a representative of the technical site management at the start and end (more critical) of all formwork and steel-fixing activities.
• Presence of a technical representative of the site management from at least one hour prior to the start of concreting works through to the end (more critical).
• Presence of the gang foreman during all formwork, steel-fixing and concreting activities, including preparatory and subsequent operations.
• Establishment of communication paths and persons to contact in the contractor's site management team and among the supervisory personnel plus an information routine concerning planning of operations, deployment of technical site management staff, supervisory personnel and gangs.

These measures appear to be unusual and elaborate as contractual provisions in

c

d

7   New Mercedes-Benz Museum, Stuttgart, Germany, 2006; architects: UN studio, van Berkel & Bos
    a,b   erecting the formwork supports
    c   erecting the formwork panels
    d   fixing the reinforcement

standard site management tasks for concreting works in construction projects. In practice it is rarely advisable to specify all these measures in the contract. However, the combination of selected factors can ease the management of building projects, even smaller ones. In particular, however, the requirements regarding the presence of supervisory personnel should always be considered if local circumstances cannot guarantee that the main contractor contractually responsible will be present during all concreting works and when much of the work is subcontracted when he will almost certainly not be present full-time.

Integration into the building contract
The measures and requirements regarding quality assurance and site management are workmanship conditions which cannot be regulated in the bill of quantities. Workmanship conditions are frequently listed in the preamble to a tender or building contract. However, the preamble is there primarily to explain the content of the tender or building contract and not to formulate contractual requirements because the legal effectiveness of contractual provisions in the preamble is not 100% certain in every legal system.
For this reason, further conditions of contract must be introduced. Existing model contracts – if available in national legislation – are useful here. For instance, in Germany VOB part B, cl. 1, para. 2 provides a very detailed example of one possible breakdown of building contract requirements into various contractual elements which are also present in the model contracts in use in the UK and elsewhere:
a) Specification
b) Special conditions of contract
c) Additional conditions of contract
d) Additional technical conditions of contract

e) General technical specifications for building works
f) General specifications for the performance of building works

The specification (which may be the bill of quantities) is a permanent element in the measurement contract. It is the key element in the building contract and the original basis for calculation and payment. However, the German VOB also recognises pre-worded, standardised contract elements which regulate specific trades (e.g. concreting works) and can be incorporated into any building contract as required. For example, the "General specifications for the performance of building works" contains a series of standards according to which concreting works can be contractually prepared, assessed and invoiced.
The structure of a building contract generally based on the German VOB is, in principle, also suitable for the clear formulation of conditions of contract outside regions covered by German legislation. The requirements regarding site management, also the aforementioned restrictions placed on qualifications and structure of personnel, can, for example, be listed in the "Special conditions of contract". Placing these regulations in a separate part of the contract lends them weight and ensures that they are observed. If placed in the preamble or other passages accompanying the contract, their effects with respect to calculating the cost of the project may go unnoticed.
The introduction of special conditions of contract to support the site management work of the designer and to safeguard the quality of workmanship also has a positive effect that goes beyond the direct supervisory effects. It indicates to potential contractors right from the tendering stage that the preparations for and the later management of the project will be

8–10 Allianz Arena, Munich, Germany, 2005; architects: Herzog & de Meuron

10

carried out especially carefully and with a high awareness of quality. This often results in less capable tenderers not even bothering to submit a tender. Furthermore, this approach equips the building contract with a series of paid organisational services to support quality which the designer's project manager can implement as required to ensure the success of the construction project.

Model contracts for monitoring quality and managing the building site may lead to uncertainty among some contractors during the tendering phase due to the initially difficult task of estimating the cost. However, once it is realised that the extra work will be paid for, the effect is put into perspective. Such contractual regulations and requirements are also helpful for the contractor's building operations because they prohibit the multiple deployment of technical personnel to a large extent and hence have a relieving effect.

The management of concreting works with the aforementioned regulations is usually very successful when resources are selected and deployed appropriately. However, this calls for an open and responsible attitude with respect to the demands of the contractor. The acceptance of these measures is achieved in everyday building operations primarily through recognition of the fact that these are fair agreements aimed at ensuring the success of all those involved.

Construction period
Difficulties in the handling of concreting works in building projects are often the result of specifying a construction period that is too short. The tendency to shorten the construction period grows in the course of the design work and contract award situation. The client's understandable desire to be able to use his structure as soon as possible often plays into the

hands of a tenderer who, in order to secure the contract, approaches the limits of feasibility when agreeing the completion date.

The designer with site management responsibilities will perhaps look anxiously at a short completion date during tendering and award of contract. However, he will regard the contractual responsibility for completing the concreting works on time as the responsibility of the contractor and frequently underestimates his share of the responsibility and the problems that can ensue within the scope of his site management duties if the construction period is too tight. Experience shows that concreting works that must be carried out under the pressure of an almost impossible completion date usually suffer from poor organisation and a repressive working environment for all those involved, and often result in inferior quality of workmanship. An adequate construction period is the foundation for the successful performance of concreting works.

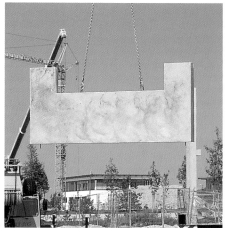

Experience and typical figures for estimating the time required for carrying out concreting works are available in the majority of design offices. Architects who essentially concentrate on design aspects generally pass on the technical planning of concreting works to the structural engineer, who will usually be able to estimate the time required as well. This rough estimate should, however, be subjected to an accurate internal check prior to informing the client. The final estimate of the construction time required should be agreed with all members of the design team, which includes the principal architect, the structural engineer and all those involved in site management. When estimating the construction time for concreting works, the following factors must be taken into account:

- If stages in the work are unknown or ambiguous in terms of their on-site operations, the associated construction times must be extended or only estimated following discussions with an external consultant.
- If much of the work is to be carried out during the cold winter months during which concreting works will be restricted because of the anticipated weather conditions at the site, then the times for the parts of the work affected should be extended. Less generous extensions are possible for compact, massive components such as foundations etc., or for sites in warmer regions. More generous extensions should be applied to components with small-format or severely fragmented geometries (walls, nibs, slender floor slabs and columns), or for sites in colder zones.
- Longer construction times should be allowed for more demanding concrete components (due to geometry, density of reinforcement, fair-face concrete, etc.).

- Concrete components with prestigious fair-face concrete surfaces always require a min. 20% extension to the construction time, and special or especially high-quality surface features can lead to a doubling of the construction time normally required. It should also be remembered here that – whenever possible – the construction of smooth fair-face concrete surfaces should not be carried out with outside temperatures < 10°C because during such conditions a distinct loss in quality is almost inevitable, even with careful workmanship. This also applies to fair-face concrete soffits.

11 a–b Erection of precast concrete wall elements for an advertising agency, Munich-Riem, Germany, 2001; architects: Amann & Gittel

Bar chart and timetable

No.	Operation	Weeks	5	10	15	20	25	30	35	40
11	Preliminary design		▬							
12	Draft design			▬▬						
13	Design for building authority approval			▬						
14	Detailed design				▬▬▬					
15	Award of contract for structure			▬▬						
16	Award of contract for fitting-out					▬▬▬				
21	Preliminary structural analysis	▬								
22	Structural analysis			▬▬						
23	Working drawings				▬▬					
31	Preparatory work					▬				
32	Structural works					▬▬▬▬				
33	Fitting-out works							▬▬▬		
41	Building authority approval				▬▬					

12

13

12 Schematic bar chart used to specify the timetable
for a building project
13 Refurbishment and modernisation works, Olympic
Stadium, Berlin, Germany, 2005; architects: von
Gerkan, Marg & Partner

Polished concrete –
Liechtenstein National Museum of Art, Vaduz

Hubertus Adam

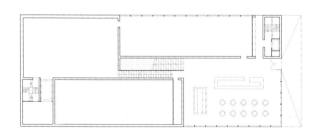

1

Design concept

Liechtenstein National Museum of Art stands in the centre of Vaduz, overlooked by the castle on the hill. Squeezed between two featureless retail and administrative buildings, the facade shimmers like an unpolished precious stone – a restrained reference to the special function of this building. Besides the works of art belonging to the Princes of Lichtenstein, the museum also houses this small country's art collection, which was started in 1968. The joint design by Meinrad Morger, Heinrich Degelo and Christian Kerez is convincing on account of its urban planning and interior layout qualities.

At the heart of this box-like edifice, which almost fills the site between two roads running east–west, is a staircase that links the two exhibition levels. This results in two options for gaining access to the first-floor exhibition rooms with their overhead lighting: the visitor either uses the central staircase which leads upwards from the foyer, or first traverses the sidelit exhibition room in the north-west corner of the building, then the adjacent exhibition room with artificial lighting before reaching an alternative staircase.

The structure of the building becomes particularly clear on the upper floor, which is lit throughout via glass ceilings. The strict rectangular plan form is divided into four exhibition rooms, also rectangular, which link up to provide a tour of the gallery. Whereas the proportions of the rooms vary, the overall size remains similar, each one having a floor area of 300–350 m². Two narrow, long rooms alternate with two wider, larger rooms – a concept which despite the identical interior design (white walls, oak parquet flooring, glass ceiling) provides astonishing variety. The exhibition rooms can be used individually, in pairs, or linked to create a total exhibition.

Liechtenstein National Museum of Art, Vaduz, 2000
Architects: Morger & Degelo, Basel,
with Christian Kerez, Zürich
Client: "Foundation for the Construction of an
Art Gallery", Vaduz
Concrete contractor: Feldmann AG, Bilten
Concrete technology: Prüftechnik HF AG, Berneck
Grinding and surface finishes contractor:
K. Studer AG, Frick

2

3

4

The effect of the exterior
The dogma of the Modern Movement –
the function of a building must be discernible from the facade – was skilfully
sidestepped by Messrs Morger, Degelo
and Kerez. Visitors to the black "Kaaba"
in Vaduz, whose only concession to iden-
tity is its name in large letters on the wall,
are amazed by the unexpectedly bright
interior. The black, reflective concrete
walls 400 mm thick present a monolithic
impression that is interrupted only by the
windows of the foyer and the sidelit exhibition room. The final grinding of the concrete resulted in a highly vigorous facade
whose effect is strengthened by the tiny
irregularities of the grinding process. The
surface almost has the texture of a fabric.
It is precisely this treatment that reduces
the monumental impact of the building
and enables it to fit in with the existing
urban environment.

The architects have succeeded in creat-
ing a building that could be described as
an integrated recluse. It exceeds the
boundaries, but remains completely faith-
ful to the prescribed building lines; it
maintains a distance to the frighteningly
trivial neighbouring buildings, but allows
them to be reflected in its facade.

Concrete surface
The surface finish of the facade was only
possible through the intensive cooperation of all those involved in the design.
The building envelope, a jointless, in situ
concrete skin, employs a specially formulated aggregate mix. Black basalt lumps
and coloured river gravel were added to
the black-pigmented cement. This was a
completely new formulation developed by
means of numerous preliminary trials, test
walls and samples.
One difficulty was that the aggregates
deviated considerably from the ideal
spherical shape. Apart from that, all the

technical requirements still had to be
maintained, e.g. stability, strength and
minimal shrinkage.
In order to achieve the desired quality for
the concrete and the surfaces, it was
important to prevent segregation during
transport and placement of the concrete.
In addition, the formwork had to be absolutely grout-tight and had to be assem-
bled with an accurate flat surface in just a
few operations. The quality of workmanship of the concreting work provided the
foundation for a good grinding result. Ten
workers took a total of five months to
grind 5–7 mm off the facade as cast,
which corresponds to about 40 tonnes of
concrete! The smooth surface was subsequently impregnated in order to enhance
the shine and also the durability.

1 Plan of ground floor, scale 1:750
2 The Liechtenstein National Museum of Art is
   situated in the centre of Vaduz below the castle.
3 Workers spent five months grinding the surface of
   the concrete with hydraulic equipment.
4 The gloss impregnation treatment lends the concrete the appearance of polished natural stone
   and at the same time protects it against graffiti.
5 Viewed close-up, individual grains of aggregate in
   the concrete mix become visible.

5

**Relief concrete –
University library, Utrecht**

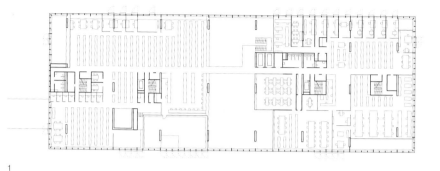

1

The university campus Uithof to the south-east of Utrecht was condensed on the basis of a masterplan by Rem Koolhaas. The library designed by Wiel Arets, from the outside an apparently massive, dark, shimmering block, forms the new hub of the campus. Connected to neighbouring buildings by means of a bridge, and in urban layout terms forming an ensemble with the new multi-storey car park, this powerful structure does not have the solitary effect one might expect to emanate from such a dominant physical presence. An auditorium, shops and an espresso bar integrate the library into the life of the campus. However, it is primarily the "experience" of the max. 33 m high reading room, which is open until late in the evening, that makes the building a popular meeting place at the heart of the university.

The facade, too, is in no way hermetic. An abstract willow tree branch motif lends the concrete surfaces a haptic quality, and in the form of silk-screen printing gives the glazing depth. The architects transferred Koolhaas' guiding principle of the "kasbah", a compact north African fortified storehouse, from the urban planning concept to the interior layout of the building. The area for the bookstacks is distributed over a dozen individual depots which float like "clouds" between the reading platforms within the block-like building. Black walls are intended to promote concentration during reading; the open interior and the large expanses of glazing ensure a bright atmosphere which inspires communication.

Design
The primary structure of the eight-storey library consists of 400 mm reinforced concrete walls with large openings on a 12.90 m grid. The 320 or 400 mm prestressed concrete hollow planks plus

University library, Utrecht, 2004
Architect: Wiel Arets, Maastricht
Client: Utrecht University
Structural engineers: ABT Adviseurs in Bouwtechniek, Arnhem/Delft
Relief concrete formwork: NOE Schaltechnik, Süssen
Facade motif: Atelier Kim Zwarts, Maastricht

2

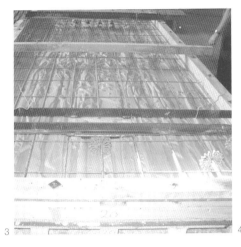

3

4

5

80 mm concrete topping make up the composite intermediate floors. In the reading room a floor load of max. 800 kg/m^2 is permissible, in the bookstacks 1300 kg/m^2. Four service cores ensure the necessary stability in the longitudinal direction, the concrete walls provide the transverse bracing. Owing to the building's considerable length of 100 m, a movement joint was included in the centre bay; the void over the hall accommodates the longitudinal movements in this central area.

Walls and columns are mainly of high-strength in situ concrete, grade B 45, although at some points compressive strength class B 65 was required. Concrete of this quality allows the walls to accommodate the high forces plus stress concentrations despite their relatively slender dimensions.
As the loadbearing structure consisted of too few identical components, the use of precast concrete elements for the structure proved uneconomic. Merely the facade panels on the external walls are precast concrete elements of grade B 35 – made possible thanks to the repetition and the fact that these panels have to carry their own weight only. The maximum size of a facade element is 1.60 x 3.45 m (width x height).

Surface relief
In order to make the content of the bookstacks visible, the walls were formed with an "embossed" pattern on the surface. The pattern used was the same one used for the silk-screen printing on the glass. Photography by the artist Kim Zwarts formed the starting point, which was abstracted to four shades of grey. As it was impossible to generate three-dimensional data from this for a CNC milling machine, the relief was cut out of a polyurethane panel by hand. In doing so, every shade of grey was allocated a cer-

tain level; the maximum depth is 25 mm. A rubber mat was cast from this relief to form a master mould, the edges of which were subsequently bevelled to make it easier to detach the rubber from the concrete. A gypsum impression of this prototype finally provided the negative mould from which the rubber form liners were produced.
However, the contractor had little experience of placing such liners in formwork for in situ concrete. Many trials were required to discover the best method of detaching the liners and, above all, the best release agent. In contrast to the calculations of the manufacturer, who had predicted four re-uses for the liners, the rubber liners could be used on average only twice for the in situ concrete. This was due to the different heights of the first two storeys, the many one-off bay sizes and the wear caused by the great number of formwork tie holes.

Colour
Whereas the design originally envisaged the use of coloured concrete, i.e. a concrete mix with pigments, there were various reasons for abandoning this concept. Experience on previous projects showed that consistent colouring could not be guaranteed. In addition, in the light of the long construction period and the enormous quantities of concrete that had to be handled on the building site, it would be difficult to guarantee a uniform shade of black for all components. And as coloured concrete is also very expensive, alternatives were investigated. In the end, the concrete was given a coat of opaque black paint after curing.

1   Plan of 6th floor, scale 1:1000
2   Relief concrete and silk-screen-printed glass surfaces alternate on the facade.
3   Horizontal formwork with rubber liners ready for the casting of precast concrete elements
4   Vertical in situ concrete formwork with rubber liners and some of the reinforcement in place
5   Striking the formwork to in situ concrete surfaces
6   Close-up view of finished relief concrete surface painted black

6

Rough texture –
youth art centre, Mouans-Sartoux

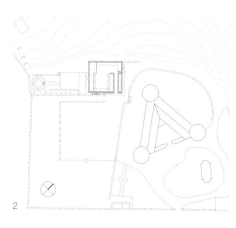

At the end of the 1980s the local authority of Mouans-Sartoux, a small French town not far from Cannes, bought the old castle and in 1990 set up a museum for concrete art. The youth centre of the L'Espace de l'Art Concret Museum was instigated later by the town's mayor and the artist Gottfried Honegger.

The supplementary facility, which enables children and young people to develop a feeling for art through theory lessons and experimentation with various techniques, was initially planned for the castle itself. However, the intended area very quickly proved to be too small. Thereupon, the architect and sculptor Marc Barani proposed an extension made up of three elements: a circular stage for open-air theatrical performances and concerts at the foot of the castle walls, an open area in the forest for sculptural work, and a building with various workshops and studios.

Design concept
The roof of the building protrudes from the slope leading up to the castle and forms a viewing platform with a view over the castle park and the surrounding forest. Enclosing fences and hardwood benches plus a pond create a place in which to relax. The new construction is separated from the old castle wall by a staircase which provides access to the studios.

The entrance area is glazed on the side facing the open-air stage and therefore helps to link interior and exterior. Contrasting with this, the other facades are essentially closed. Only the side facing the park is punctuated by small openings of different sizes and formats, offering specific views over the park. Nevertheless, the interior is bright, thanks to the use of glass blocks and a glass bottom to the pond on the rooftop terrace, both of which allow plenty of daylight to reach into the far corners of the art studios.

Surfaces
To contrast with the random rubble stone masonry of the castle walls, the fair-face concrete surfaces have an especially smooth finish. Only the facade facing the park was given an especially rough texture. In order to achieve this special surface finish, additional, 100 mm wide, sand-blasted pinewood boards were laid in the formwork. To prevent joints disrupting the texture, the formwork for the entire wall measuring 18 × 4 m was set up in one piece. Different thicknesses and small gaps between the formwork boards mean that every individual board used is now clearly visible in the finished wall. This technique resulted in a vigorous surface which emphasizes the dialogue between the new building and the historic random rubble stone masonry of the castle walls.

Youth art centre, Mouans-Sartoux, 1998
Architects: Atelier Barani, Nice
Client: Mouans-Sartoux local authority,
Alpes Maritimes
Structural engineers: Dinatech, Mouans-Sartoux
Main structure contractor:
Savonitto, Roquefort-Les-Pins

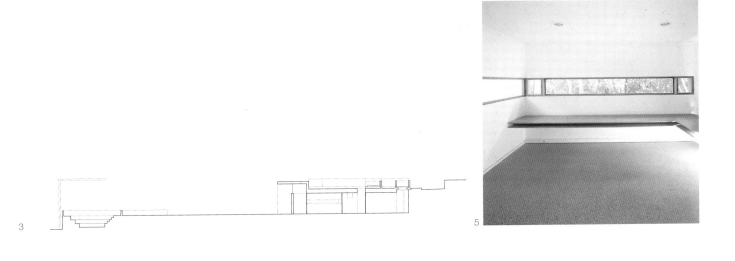

3

5

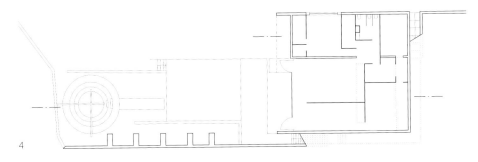

4

1   Entrance facade
2   Location plan, scale 1:2000
3   Section, scale 1:500
4   Plan, scale 1:500
5   Studio for computer art
6   Rough surface texture of park facade

6

Fair-face concrete

The design of fair-face concrete structures

Andreas Meck
Susanne Frank

Hardly any other building material leaves more of a mark on the appearance of our surroundings than concrete. It is primarily the structural carcass for which concrete is accepted as an inevitable building material. But the situation is different when "carcass" is the same as "skin", i.e. we are dealing with fair-face concrete surfaces.

"Will it stay like that?" Quite often, the architect is confronted with just such a question. The incredulous observer assumes that the exposed concrete surface represents some kind of interim condition, and that the surface will be plastered or painted.

Unintentionally, or so it seems, the associations that concrete evokes in its use for the structural carcass – unfinished and coarse, pragmatic and less atmospheric – are transferred to exposed concrete surfaces deliberately designed to be just that. But is the issue here really the material itself or rather the fact that we assume concrete, frequently used purely as a construction material or a loadbearing material, has no potential whatsoever for use as an architectural device? Perhaps this notion is also based on the fact that concrete can be – and is – used for everything, but frequently without thinking. The "concrete jungle" expression did not just arise for nothing.
Nevertheless, is concrete really "just" durable, cheap, clean, zero-maintenance and practical? In contrast to the pragmatic aspects, the numerous design options for concrete rarely share the limelight, although there are many impressive examples that demonstrate the sensual qualities that concrete surfaces can possess.

For example, Le Corbusier proved in impressive fashion how concrete can be used splendidly for the sculptural, artistic design of buildings (fig. 1). In conjunction with the lighting effects, the rough surfaces of his *béton brut* radiate strength and sensuality.
Or Tadao Ando, whose surfaces produced with smooth formwork give his buildings a velvet-like finish (fig. 2), providing a high degree of haptic effects and poesy, e.g. the leaves laid in the formwork to his conference pavilion in Weil am Rhein (fig. 5).
The Swiss architects Jacques Herzog and Pierre de Meuron used printed concrete and glass surfaces on their design for the library in Eberswalde. The overall printing unifies the surfaces and appears to cancel out the differences between concrete and glass (fig. 3).
The work of Eduardo Chillida can be included in this context. His impressive, large concrete sculptures show how to handle the material from the viewpoint of the artist and sculptor.

Sensuality, poesy and atmosphere
The aforementioned examples prove that the appearance of concrete embody strength, expressiveness and a sensual, poetical quality – whenever the material is employed with circumspection and in an architectural–artistic sense.
It would be difficult at this point to present all conceivable variations and possibilities regarding fair-face concrete surfaces. The spectrum is enormous and the "sensational" in new approaches is readily to hand in every trade journal.

Instead, our approach here will be to evaluate the diversity of fair-face concrete in relation to its significance for the architectural concept. How is the appearance of a building affected by the design of its surface? How is a design idea conveyed?

The projects have one thing in common: they are all made from in situ concrete.

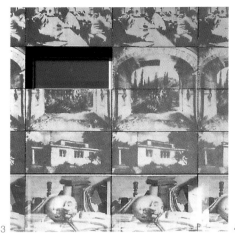

However, the conditions and the design intentions are totally different. We will explain why the respective project was implemented in concrete with that particular surface finish, and what the architect was aiming to achieve by using concrete. The designs are presented in conjunction with the underlying concept. And the context always plays a major role here.

Every building exists in a relationship with its surroundings. The design of the building, its form, it proportions and the configuration of its interior and exterior are responses to this environment.

Likewise, social and historical circumstances influence the design process. The realisation of an architectural concept, i.e. an image or an idea, means dealing with the materiality, recognising the connection between form and material. A building must fit in as a whole. The design of its surfaces provides the fine-tuning and precision. The finished surfaces convey haptic and sensual qualities.

Concrete – fair-face concrete

What do we understand by "fair-face concrete"?
In principle, a concrete building can exist in two conditions. It is either rough, i.e. unfinished, the structural carcass as the "basic form of the construction", or it is finished. It is in this latter situation that we speak of fair-face concrete.
These two basic forms differ in one way. When using concrete purely as a building material for the structural carcass, the external appearance of the building experiences a major transformation because the loadbearing primary construction undergoes "subsequent treatment", i.e. the facades are clad. Thereafter, the concrete is no longer visible. The situation is

different when the concrete remains on show as the finished surfaces. In some cases it is still loadbearing, but at the same time it is still the visible material of the external skin: fair-face concrete.

The concrete mix is fundamental to the appearance of the concrete surface, and this is determined by the choice of cement, aggregates and additives/admixtures, e.g. the addition of pigments to colour the concrete. Depending on the designer's intentions, a fair-face concrete surface can also be subsequently treated and refined.
The design of the surface, the "skin" of the building, has a crucial influence on its character. It is therefore no wonder that this topic attracts so much attention. What this means for the technological realisation is that the quality of the finished surface is determined by the concrete mix, the quality and characteristics of the formwork panels and also the nature of any subsequent treatment. The following factors in the production process influence the look of the finished surface:

- the concrete mix together with the type of cement, aggregates and additives/admixtures
- the surface texture of the formwork materials
- the joints (in the formwork and in the concrete)
- the formwork tie holes, which after striking the formwork should ideally present a regular pattern

In order that the finished building corresponds to the architectural concept, a fair-face concrete facade requires careful, precise advance planning.

1 Monastery of La Tourette, Eveux, 1960; architect: Le Corbusier
2 Koshino House, Ashinga, 1979-81; architect: Tadao Ando
3 Printed fair-face concrete facade (photoconcrete), forestry management library, Eberswalde, 1999; architects: Herzog & de Meuron
4 Residential development, Lyon, 1994; architects: Jourda & Perraudin
5 Fair-face concrete surface with leaves laid in the formwork, Vitra conference pavilion, Weil am Rhein, 1993; architect: Tadao Ando

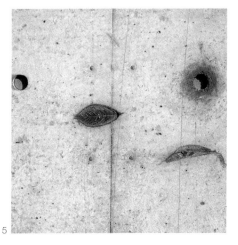

**Parish centre and youth club,
Thalmässing**

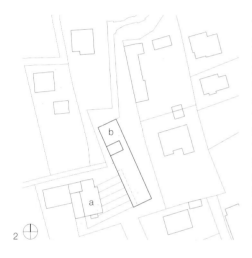

The design of this parish centre and youth club should be seen in the context of an important existing building. The parish of Thalmässing has a small, but in terms of its architecture and details, very charming, old parish church located on the side of a hill. In terms of its height and position, the new parish centre respects the importance of the church as a purposeful, dominant edifice. The appearance of the new building and its use of materials are modest and leave colour and ornamentation to the church itself. There is an open square between the centre, the club and the church, and this links the different buildings to form a coherent group. The full width of the parish hall and foyer is glazed on the church side.

The block-like building otherwise has very few windows. This plainness is relieved by a deep recess on the side facing the square. This places old and new in juxtaposition, the church facade forming a boundary and gives the parish hall breadth, purpose and affinity.

The external, smooth facade of the build-

ing contrasts with the texture of the materials of the interior surfaces, which are mainly clad in oak panelling. Fine wickerwork lends the interior of the parish hall a warm atmosphere.

Monolith with homogeneous surface
The building's simplicity and obviousness radiates calmness and composure. This monolithic structure, completely in concrete, achieves its strength through sublimation and does not compete with the church.

A few precise openings give the block a sculptural quality. Its velvety smooth surfaces appear tranquil and homogeneous. In order to realise the design concept, an appearance devoid of any pattern was required and unavoidable joints had to be relegated to the background.

This represented a challenge for the planning and production of the concrete. The desire for a monolithic appearance is apparently a contradiction in terms because concreting always entails working in segments (pours, lifts) – a procedure that leaves marks.

Parish centre and youth club, Thalmässing, 2004
Architects: meck architekten, Munich
Client: Diocese of Eichstätt, parish community of Thalmässing
Structural engineers: Ingenieurbüro Hans-Ludwig Haushofer, Markt Schwaben
Concrete contractor: ARLT, Nördlingen

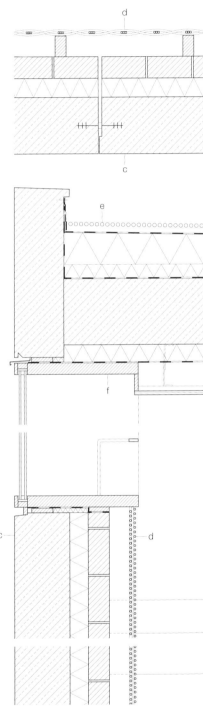

4

c

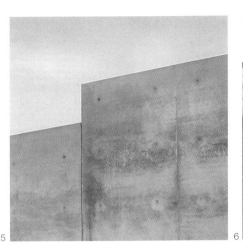

5

6

d

e

f

c   d

7

This difficulty was overcome on the parish centre by using large-format formwork panels with a smooth face which on this low-rise building enabled horizontal joints to be avoided altogether. Besides a consistent arrangement of the formwork panels over the surface, care was taken at the design stage to ensure that the formwork tie holes were regularly spaced over the entire facade.

The lengths of the concrete pours coincided with the vertical joints in the formwork. The individual sections were cast continuously over the full height to avoid horizontal construction joints.
To do this, ground slabs and intermediate floors were suspended between the external walls concreted in one operation – an unusual procedure. The careful treatment of the joints required in the structure had to be carefully planned at the design stage because these generally represent a distinct visual interruption.
The expansion joints, which in this case are determined by the properties of the subsoil, also had to play a subsidiary role with respect to the overall appearance. On the outside they are visible only as razor-thin slits in the concrete surface, which were produced with a diamond saw after striking the formwork. These slits, just 4 mm wide, always coincide with the formwork joints. On the inside, the wall was cast with a recess to match the full 20 mm joint width required by the design (figs 4 and 5).

Abstraction, reduction
The monolithic effect of the building is strengthened and disruptive details are avoided.
The parapet for example is a special design because the normal detail – leaving the front edge of the sheet metal capping visible – could not be reconciled with the architectural concept.

But the parapet detail still had to satisfy the requirements of the construction – fixing for the roof waterproofing and protection to prevent ingress of water – and also had to be invisible from the outside. Instead of using an additional, new material to cover the parapet, the roof edge was also cast in concrete. Additional compaction of the upper lifts of concrete in the region of the parapet achieved a higher density in the concrete microstructure and hence a better waterproofing effect. For additional protection, the top surface (which slopes inwards) was primed and given several coats of an impregnation treatment, whereas the sides remained untreated.

1 View from south
2 Location plan, scale 1:2000
   a parish church of St Peter and St Paul
   b parish centre and youth club
3 View from north-west
4 Horizontal section through facade showing vertical expansion joint, scale 1:20
5 Vertical expansion joint
6 Internal view of external wall
7 Vertical section through facade, scale 1:20
   c Wall construction: 300 mm fair-face concrete
      thermal insulation, 100 mm cellular glass
      115 mm clay brickwork inner leaf
   d wickerwork on timber frame
   e Roof construction:
      50 mm gravel
      waterproofing, polyolefin sheeting
      thermal insulation with integral falls, expanded polystyrene foam, 90–240 mm
      vapour barrier, bitumen sheeting
      350 mm reinforced concrete
      thermal insulation, 100 mm cellular glass
      vapour barrier
      suspended ceiling, 20 mm oak with glaze finish
   f oak lining (glaze finish) to window reveals

Cemetery complex, Munich

In contrast to the parish centre and youth club in Thalmässing, this complex is located in an urban environment that offered little incentive for an interesting design.

The plot, a former car park with waste collection depot, is surrounded by allotments and an industrial estate, and is not far from a busy motorway. A more worthy location for a chapel of rest had first to be created.

The new cemetery complex opposite the entrance to the existing, old cemetery is arranged as a strict, almost monastery-like square on the edge of a landscaped park. Together with the coarse enclosing walls, the simple, distinct lines of the structure form a place of peace.

Three courtyards define the complex. Paths to the cemetery, the chapel of rest, the laying-out cells and the entrance to the old cemetery lead off from the central, quiet entrance courtyard.

The chapel of rest shelters beneath a concrete canopy. The chapel itself is a box of smooth oak, which forms a counterweight to the stone floors and the rough courtyard walls of coursed rubble stone.

The atmosphere in the chapel interior is dominated by the warm colour of the enclosing timber walls and has a contempletive, sacred character thanks to the avoidance of a direct view to the outside. A golden shimmering water effect catches the eye and gives the room a special light and meditative atmosphere.

The "stone"

The complex is conceived as a heavy-weight element "rising up out of the earth". Oak, weathering steel and, primarily, the "stone" (fair-face concrete and natural stone) determine the overall appearance.

The sculpted forms radiate tranquillity, dignity and composure. Visible from afar in this open landscape, the long-span "stone" roof is a distinctive element.

The sculpted buildings with their homogenous surfaces are built in reinforced concrete, the properties of which correspond ideally to the concept of this structure because this material can be moulded into virtually any shape.

Large spans are also no problem in reinforced concrete. The image of the long-span "stone" canopy can only really be achieved with this material.

Cemetery complex, Munich, 2000
Architects: Andreas Meck (meck architekten) and Stephan Köppel, Munich
Client: MRG, Munich
Structural engineer: Dieter Herrschmann, Munich
Fair-face concrete consultant: Bauberatung Zement, Munich
Concrete contractor: Hoser, Markt Schwaben

Differentiated surfaces
Concrete provides the chance of differentiating surfaces according to architectural requirements – another material property crucial to the realisation of this design.

Different types of surface finish can be achieved depending on the type of formwork panels used and the subsequent treatment of the concrete, enabling a rise in quality from outside to inside, and from rough to smooth.

The external surfaces of the chapel of rest and the adjoining central courtyard are in coarse, homogenous fair-face concrete, which has been given its texture by means of bush-hammering. This mechanical treatment exposes the aggregate in the concrete so that the surfaces are given a uniform appearance. The increased concrete cover to the reinforcement must be considered at the design stage, otherwise such subsequent mechanical treatment is not possible. By revealing the aggregates in the concrete, bush-hammering gives a concrete surface the character of a gravestone worked by a stonemason.

The concrete surfaces facing inwards have a board-marked finish – a linear pattern achieved by using a formwork of boards with a highly absorbent surface. The imprint of the rough-sawn boards lends the concrete a vigorous texture and creates a visual reference to the more noble oak wood lining to the chapel of rest.

Inside the chapel, the materials are used differently depending on their visual and haptic qualities. Both the timber and the concrete here have smooth surfaces. The concrete was cast against smooth formwork panels with a mildly absorbent surface.

In the passageway to the laying-out cells, the concrete surfaces with which the bereaved come into direct contact were ground after hardening to give them a more refined finish.

Ageing with dignity
All the materials used are solid and left untreated. Their natural ageing over the course of time is deliberate and part of the architectural concept – a reference to

the theme of mortality. The stone sculpture ages "with dignity" in keeping with the purpose of this complex.

1   View from east, facade of bush-hammered concrete
2   Location plan, scale 1:5000
3   Internal courtyard looking towards chapel of rest
4   Bell tower (in background) and courtyard bell structure (foreground), rough-sawn board finish
5   Chapel of rest, oak walls beneath a canopy of bush-hammered concrete
6   Passageway with laying-out cells, rough-sawn board finish, ground concrete finish to low-level walls

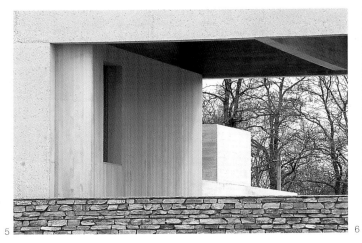

Library and lecture theatre building, Weimar

The design of the new library and lecture theatre building belonging to the Bauhaus University in Weimar is dominated by reference to the historical buildings of the town and the concept of being inserted into the existing built environment of the town centre.

The plot, formerly an industrial site not open to the public, is in close proximity to the historical heart of Weimar with its famous Goethe House. Following the unification of Germany in 1989, the town was given the chance to restructure the area and re-integrate it into the town centre in conjunction with the demolition of existing building stock not worthy of preservation.

The building is shaped like a "V" on plan, which permits new spatial references within the block. One leg of the "V" is reserved for the library, whose glazed facade faces onto an open square within the block – the University Forum. The other leg is for offices, which face onto a quiet internal courtyard.

Footpaths running north-south and east-west plus a series of public squares and yards link the plot with the town centre. The lecture theatre is integrated into the

change in ground level, which drops towards the north end of the site. This results in two access zones, one on the library level, the other in front of the lecture theatre.

"Make-up piece"
The new structure fits into the existing urban context like a "make-up piece", but at the same time breaks free of the block. The five-storey library makes its presence felt with a distinct gesture in the streetscape of Steubenstrasse. It is visible from afar as a modern public building within the historic core of the town.

The design of the library reminds the observer of bookshelves. The building looks like a large frame (the bookcase) within which the rows of shelving are set up like books on shelves. Wood lines the complete interior, corresponding to the "wooden library" of the old Anna Amalia library nearby, which was also a wooden insertion within a solid structure.

"Stretched skin"
Several aspects favoured the use of concrete for this building, including structural reasons. The realisation of the "bookshelves" idea and the large internal

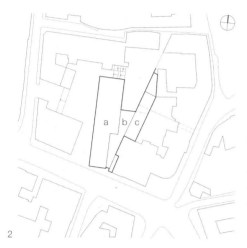

Library and lecture theatre, Weimar, 2005
Architects: Andreas Meck (meck architekten) and Stephan Köppel (phases 1–4), Munich
Client: Free State of Thuringia, represented by Erfurt Building Authority
Structural engineers: Pabst & Partner Ingenieure, Weimar
Painting and making good: Reinhard Bergener, Niederorschel

3 a

b

4

volume of the lecture theatre called for long spans, which are readily possible in reinforced concrete. Concrete also suited the notion of a "make-up piece" because the material is cast in situ and therefore is ideal for "filling the gap". Another good reason for choosing this building material was the design of the facade in the context of its historical environs. Rendered timber-frame structures in which the construction beneath the skin of render can still be detected are typical of Weimar. These facades have interesting surfaces with a special architectural charm because the layers that make up the construction remain discernible. The new building interprets this traditional theme in a contemporary manner. Fair-face concrete is employed throughout, but without any special requirements for the surface quality – a solution dictated by both architectural and economic reasons. After striking the formwork, the rough surfaces were worked only to the extent of filling holes and grinding down protrusions, leaving a vigorous surface with minor irregularities. The casting of the concrete is revealed, likewise the "signatures" of the workers who made good the surface afterwards. The treatment of the facade is similar to that of a sculptor working a

piece of stone, who hammers away all disruptive elements and produces others. Like the historical facades in which the timber members can still be identified beneath the skin of render, the exposed concrete structure reflects the method of construction of the new building.

"Material exposure" and colours
The vigorous texture of the concrete surface gives the facade its special quality. A dark grey glaze was applied which allows the surface underneath to remain visible and preserves the fact that subsequent treatment of the surface was only local. Like the render on the historical building stock, the surface looks like a "stretched skin". The dark grey glaze reinforces the reference to the historical urban setting.

5

c

6

1 View from Steubenstrasse
2 Location plan, scale 1:2500
   a library and lecture theatre
   b entrance and foyer
   c offices
3 Surface finish to facade
   a concrete surface after striking formwork, partially made good
   b concrete surface cleaned, some areas ground flat
   c finished concrete surface, primed with an etching solution, mineral glaze finish coat
4 Historical facade
5 View from south
6 Staircase in foyer, concrete surfaces made good after striking and given a glaze finish

Fair-face concrete surfaces

Fair-face concrete is not always simply fair-face concrete. Every surface exhibits its own qualities depending on concrete mix, formwork and subsequent treatment. The selection shown here provides an insight into the options regarding concept, working and treatment of fair-face concrete surfaces (figs 2–8). The examples on pp. 74–79 also show the diversity of the finished product.

Primarily, it is the concrete mix that determines the colour and shade, but so can the underlying structure. Depending on the desired effect, this can be influenced by the choice of aggregate or the addition of pigments or by using other cements. The formwork – a negative imprint – essentially determines the texture of the surface as cast. The variations stretch from rough to smooth depending on the materials used and their pretreatment; structures and patterns are transferred to the concrete. Furthermore, joints between the formwork panels and formwork tie holes can generate a deliberate pattern (fig. 1).

Finally, fair-face concrete surfaces can also be worked after casting and striking to create any type of structure or texture or pattern to suit the architectural demands.

1   Fair-face concrete surfaces, smooth panels (bottom) and rough-sawn boards (top), swimming pool, Arzúa, 2001; architects: Antonio Raya, Carlos Quintáns, Cristóbal Crespo, La Coruña
2   Rough-sawn, unplaned boards, grey cement
3   Transparent glaze, mineral paint
4   Sawn, coloured concrete, light aggregate, white cement
5   Pitched, limestone aggregate, grey cement
6   Exposed aggregate finish, coloured aggregate with rounded grains, grey cement
7   Polished concrete surface, light and dark aggregates, white cement
8   Different surface treatments but with the same concrete mix
    a   smooth formwork
    b   sand-blasted
    c   lightly brushed and washed
    d   acid-etched
    e   comb-chiselled
    f   pointed

1

2

3

4

5

6

7

8 a

b

c

d

e

f

Fair-face concrete – design and construction

Martin Peck

Fair-face concrete is a concrete with special demands placed on the appearance of its surface. And the appearance of an exposed concrete surface can vary considerably depending on the method of construction. Surfaces can reflect the formwork, can be worked manually after striking the formwork, or can be treated in a number of other ways. It is hardly reasonable to explain the whole spectrum of architectural possibilities because preferred surface features depend on architectural fashions and change from time to time.

The situation is different with the large-scale utility structures of civil or hydraulic engineering, where exposed concrete surfaces are part and parcel of the typical forms of construction and are not usually expected to satisfy any challenging architectural concepts. But in prestigious superstructures, the fair-face concrete surface is frequently a key architectural design element.
Fashions have always dictated that the favoured surface textures change over the years. Developments in formwork and formwork panels, originally motivated purely by economic considerations, were among the prime movers in the evolution of fair-face concrete. The appearance of coated plywood panels in the 1960s, which enabled the economic realisation of large concrete surfaces, eventually led to the smooth, virtually unblemished exposed concrete surfaces which have been popular since around 1980. However, the production of fair-face concrete surfaces with a smooth, non-absorbent formwork panel is, even today, regarded as the "zenith" of concrete construction and is still difficult to control in terms of work required, costs and results. The production of fair-face concrete embodies a series of characteristic problems that cannot be entirely eliminated even when great care is taken. Nevertheless, the realisation of impressive fair-face concrete structures for museums, theatres, government and other buildings has led to widespread acceptance of this method of construction and the increasing use of fair-face concrete surfaces for churches, schools and private-sector utility and office buildings.

The architect in his role as chief designer often understands the production of a fair-face concrete component very differently to the contractor who has to build it. From the architect's point of view, the production of the constructional properties of

components and the on-site planning are obviously parts of the contractor's brief. For the architect, it is his design concept and the authentic realisation of his ideas that are paramount. The constructional, perhaps even permanently invisible, components of the structure and the properties of those components are, for the architect, merely the supporting structure, the underlying substance behind his design. For the contractor, the planning of on-site operations, the organisation of the technical procedures and the choice of methods are the most important factors and represent the main part of his workload. The contractual requirement regarding the production of specified surface features are, for the contractor, always "secondary" to the constructional aspects and are often not attributed their real importance until the architect's ideas do not come to fruition and the contractor is threatened with financial penalties.

These underlying attitudes have led to a need for advice and technical rules. Many countries have therefore tried to produce codes of practice to assist the design and construction of fair-face concrete. In Germany and Austria, such efforts resulted in technical data sheets and standards being published in the 1990s, which contain provisions for the design, construction and assessment of fair-face concrete surfaces. Indeed, in Austria surface qualities are classified and defined by way of individual criteria and properties. The German-language codes of practice are as follows:

- The data sheet "Sichtbeton", published jointly by the Deutscher Beton- & Bautechnikverein e.V. (DBV) and the Bundesverband der Deutschen Zementindustrie e.V. (BDZ)
- The directive "Geschalte Betonflächen" ("Sichtbeton") published by the Österreichische Vereinigung für Beton- & Bautechnik (ÖVBB)

These codes of practice have been revised several times to reflect changing legal and technical parameters. In fact, in 2004 the German data sheet was adapted – in terms of structure and content – to match its Austrian counterpart to such an extent that an essentially coherent set of rules is now available, at least for German-speaking countries.

1 Smooth fair-face concrete surfaces produced with non-absorbent formwork panels, crematorium, Berlin, 1998; architects: Axel Schultes Architekten

Concept, realisation and reality
Normally, the architect decides on the surface features of a fair-face concrete structure as part of his overall architectural concept. The architectural design must satisfy, in the first place, the following boundary conditions:

- The draft design for the planned structure takes into account the ideas and specifications of the client with regard to the intended use and any basic design or material related ideas. The location of the structure within the existing built environment or landscape and any restrictions this might impose must also be considered.
- However, the draft design and all its details are subject to the demands of feasibility ("buildability"), which must be considered with direct reference to the budget and the building technology options. The architect must therefore possess adequate basic knowledge to be able to realise whether, how and with what technical means his design can be implemented, and what degree of success can be expected. This requires the designer to have a basic knowledge about materials technology and building operations.

When designing fair-face concrete surfaces, the surface features should be assessed at an early stage of the design with regard to their production, costs and probable success. It is not difficult to write a technical specification of the works required to produce a reinforced concrete component, which normally entails specifying three main parameters: component dimensions, concrete properties and amount of reinforcement. Such features can be specified unambiguously with little effort (standards, working drawings, dimensions, etc.). And most of these constructional details are specified not by the architect, but instead by the structural engineer.

In contrast to this, specifying the requirements for the appearance of fair-face concrete surfaces is the job of the architect and is far more complicated. The architect has to convey his design concept and not simply reproduce measurable and calculable technical parameters. But the designer's ideas regarding the appearance and effect of a fair-face concrete surface have their origins in creative thoughts, which are not covered by clauses in standards and may not even be related to the framework conditions of

materials and production. A lack of explicit, generally accepted features and terms applying to building with fair-face concrete forces the designer to improvise when specifying his requirements. It is for this reason that the unambiguous contractual specification of fair-face concrete is frequently unsuccessful in practice and leads to differences of opinion regarding the contractual targets. Furthermore, the designer often underestimates the work (costs) and the risks involved in the realisation of fair-face concrete surfaces and neglects his own input in the process. In addition, the contractual performance conditions are often written unfavourably. Even in the case of high quality expectations, the decision about who is awarded the contract is mostly decided on the basis of the lowest price.

Data sheet as design aid
It has already become clear that design concepts cannot and should not be either standardised or straitjacketed by codes of practice. However, it is usually the case that the surface features intended are neither completely new nor extraordinary. Instead, the design ideas are mostly variations within long-term architectural trends. Therefore, it can be beneficial and sensible to standardise the terms for known, common design and construction requirements, and to provide appropriate regulations. This is the idea behind the German DBV/BDZ data sheet on fair-face concrete and the equivalent Austrian ÖVBB directive, both of which provide the designer with standardised parameters and key terms so that the required features of an exposed surface are underpinned by proper technical requirements and criteria. Following its revision and republication in 2004, the German DBV/BDZ data sheet represents the most up-to-date and most comprehensive code of practice in Europe covering the design, construction and assessment of fair-face concrete; the content of this data sheet therefore forms the basis of the following observations.

Terms
The technical communication between client, designer and contractor calls for a generally acknowledged set of key terms. The technical codes of practice help us here by providing definitions of certain terms.

Building with fair-face concrete often suffers because there is a lack of standardised definitions, which results in the use of vague terms and ambiguities in contracts or specifications and, in the end, during practical everyday building operations. The term "fair-face concrete" stems from a valid but outdated German standard (DIN 18217), which describes fair-face concrete as a "concrete surface with requirements regarding its appearance". But this definition carries little weight and can be interpreted in all sorts of ways. For a long time, this deficit led to an almost arbitrary use of the term "fair-face concrete" in building contracts in Germany, with the features desired seldom being adequately defined. The German DBV/BDZ data sheet expands and fine-tunes the term "fair-face concrete" by defining two basic categories:

- Fair-face concrete with low requirements defines exposed concrete surfaces that meet the assessment criteria and the design and construction conditions of fair-face concrete class SB 1.
- Fair-face concrete with normal or high requirements defines exposed concrete surfaces according to the assessment criteria and the design and construction conditions of fair-face concrete classes SB 2, SB 3 and SB 4.

In contrast to the ambiguous definition in DIN 18217, the above definitions are founded on clear, in some cases measurable, technical criteria which, when in doubt, can be verified (or otherwise) to provide a clear factual classification. It is also an advantage that the categories differentiate not only between two qualities, but instead define the fair-face concrete as a whole and hence specify a lower assessment limit. According to the data sheet, concrete surfaces that do not attain class SB 1 cannot be classified as fair-face concrete.

The ambiguous term "sample panel" has also been redefined because the contractual effectiveness of a sample panel had not been regulated precisely hitherto. In the majority of cases all trial panels were called sample panels irrespective of their contractual significance. The data sheet therefore distinguishes between trial panels and reference panels, and both types of panel must be considered in conjunction with building operations (fig. 3):

- Trial panels are surfaces on which trials are carried out for two reasons:
  1. The contractor can carry out these trials in order to optimise his technical procedures. If this is not called for in the contract, the ensuing costs are generally borne by the contractor. The contractor can minimise the work and costs by carrying out the trials on components whose appearance is irrelevant (basement walls, plant rooms, etc.), provided he obtains the consent of the client.
  2. If the building contract requires the production of trial panels in order to coordinate the contractual requirements between the parties involved or to specify the appearance of the surfaces, this work is regulated by the contract and must be paid for accordingly. In this case trial panels are usually specially produced on the building site, do not form any part of the building and are disposed of after completing the fair-face concrete works.
- Reference panels are exposed surfaces that provide a binding contractual definition of the desired appearance. They are selected from suitable trial panels. In this case it is important to consider the properties of the panel as a whole. One or more panels can be referred to in the contract. Reference panels specify the contractual performance in a practical manner. But they assume the status of a binding contractual provision only after both parties to the contract have acknowledged their surface features unanimously in writing and from that time onwards they represent the due contractual target. They are valid as the contractual reference component for comparative assessments when inspecting and accepting fair-face concrete surfaces in the project.

The detailed specification of contractual requirements regarding the appearance of exposed surfaces through the production of trial panels and subsequent selection of reference panels is a simple and fair method which is explained in more detail in the following discussion of the precontractual and contractual specification of fair-face concrete works. It releases the client and the designer from the task of explaining the desired appearance of surfaces in the tender documents and the building contract by way of improvised formulations but nevertheless eliminates the danger of an inadequate specification. Furthermore, the ideas of the designer are placed alongside the practical feasibility, which allows design ideas to "mature" and prevents surprises and disappointments when assessing the

2 Data sheet for fair-face concrete (German only) published jointly by Deutscher Beton- & Bautechnik Verein e.V. and Bundesverband der Deutschen Zementindustrie e.V., Berlin /Düsseldorf, 2004

Merkblatt Sichtbeton

Merkblatt Sichtbeton

Fassung August 2004

DEUTSCHER BETON- UND
BAUTECHNIK-VEREIN E.V.

BUNDESVERBAND DER
DEUTSCHEN ZEMENTINDUSTRIE E.V.

2

3

first exposed surfaces as required by the contract. However, in order to rule out an inappropriate or indeed wrongful use of the reference panels approach, the German DBV/BDZ data sheet on fair-face concrete specifies a few conditions:

• The reference panels must comply with the requirements regarding the appearance of exposed surfaces as stated in the specification, tender documents and building contract and such requirements must form the basis of their selection. This is intended to protect the contractor in the case of trial panels which, due to particularly favourable circumstances, exhibit a quality that clearly exceeds that demanded by the contract and which cannot be reliably reproduced or the costs of which are incalculable. Such surfaces may be used as contractual reference panels only with the express agreement of the contractor.
• Trial panels on the structure whose viewing distances and lighting conditions cannot be kept constant over the period of assessment (e.g. internal walls in confined or window-less rooms, basement walls) or those not on the building site or in its immediate vicinity are unsuitable as contractual reference panels.
• Surfaces on existing structures are very good for illustrating the design ideas in the course of tendering (e.g. photos, site visits). However, such surfaces may not be used as contractual reference panels because
  1. this is an unacceptable selection from the overall quality of the existing structure,
  2. the building materials and methods of production are generally unknown and the contractor cannot establish them, and
  3. the influences affecting the ageing of the surfaces (especially their appearance) that has occurred in the meantime are unknown and such effects cannot be considered when producing new concrete components.

The German DBV/BDZ data sheet on fair-face concrete recommends, in conjunction with fair-face concrete classes, that trial panels be considered in the contract when exposed surfaces of classes SB 2 and SB 3 are required. If class SB 4 surfaces are required, the data sheet prescribes trial panels in the contract. Classes for fair-face concrete surfaces were defined in the course of adapting

the German DBV/BDZ data sheet to match the contents of the Austrian directive.

Fair-face concrete classes
The fair-face concrete classes contain comprehensive information for the design and construction of the surface features of the respective class. However, it cannot be assumed that the respective surface quality would necessarily be achieved just by adhering to the specification. The construction conditions for the respective fair-face concrete class are merely the prerequisites necessary to achieve the desired quality according to the current level of knowledge. But this is not always sufficient without corresponding care or prior trials.

The choice and specification of a fair-face concrete class does not establish a clear level of quality, but instead formulates construction conditions and individual criteria for assessing the result. It is the overall appearance of the actual surface as built that really counts, and this is the product of the materials and methods used and must be compared with the contractual provisions. The overall impression therefore always takes precedence over the individual criteria because the architect can only compare his ideas and expectations regarding a fair-face concrete surface with its overall appearance. If a surface is contractually acceptable in terms of its overall impression, then the individual criteria do not need to be assessed.

Fair-face concrete classes and examples of components
Table 1 of the DBV/BDZ data sheet lists four fair-face concrete classes SB 1 to SB 4 (fig. 5). Every class includes examples of components, assessment criteria (individual criteria) and construction advice. The individual criteria are defined by means of abbreviations which are explained in detail in tables 2 and 4 of the data sheet. Further regulations concerning the design, construction and assessment of exposed surfaces can be found in the text of the data sheet and in further tables.

The classification begins with fair-face concrete class SB 1. This specifies the lowest level of quality, which is described as "concrete surfaces with low architectural requirements" and gives "basement walls or areas for primarily commercial uses" as examples of components. Such

3 Trial and reference panel, Richard Rother School, Kitzingen, 2006; architects: röschert + schäfer volkach architekten + ingenieure
4 Concrete surfaces satisfying high architectural requirements (SB 3), technical grammar school, Bagnols-sur-Cèze, France, 1999; architect: Jacques Brion

examples characterise areas in buildings that normally require only a minimum standard and are designed and constructed without any significant architectural input. Class SB 1 is necessary to define the lowest quality level for fair-face concrete; below this standard, fair-face concrete is not defined. This definition has a distinct effect on ambiguous contractual formulations. For example, this definition means that a contractual requirement regarding "fair-face concrete" that is not specified in any more detail will be built to the SB 1 standard.

Fair-face concrete class SB 2 is defined as "concrete surfaces with normal architectural requirements" and gives "staircase towers and retaining walls" as typical examples, i.e. areas exposed to public gaze. Such surfaces should therefore comply with the requirements for a certain inconspicuousness and consistency. Class SB 2 therefore also describes a minimum quality without any special architectural intentions.

Fair-face concrete class SB 3 contains regulations for concrete surfaces with "high architectural requirements, e.g. facades to buildings" (fig. 4). This class covers those surfaces of components that are designed to achieve certain architectural aims but are not expected to reach the upper levels of feasibility. The majority of concrete surfaces specified as "fair-face concrete" these days fall into this category.

Fair-face concrete class SB 4 specifies "concrete surfaces with special architectural significance" (fig. 6), i.e. "prestigious components in buildings". Class SB 4 in principle therefore complies with the intention of class SB 3 but is coupled with an especially demanding architectural brief and high expectations regarding how well the results match the design concept. Class SB 4 applies to building tasks that are particularly demanding in terms of design and construction.

Fair-face concrete classes SB 3 and SB 4 specify and regulate exposed surfaces for which the realisation of the appearance as demanded by the contract has a priority and the design intentions should be fulfilled as accurately as possible. The constructional character of the concrete component is less important than the architectural effect of its exposed surfaces. This principle is valid for both

4

classes, but is simply applied more strictly for class SB 4 than for class SB 3.

Individual criteria

Individual criteria, designated by abbreviations, are assigned to the various fair-face concrete classes (fig. 5). The abbreviations are supplemented by numbers to designate the gradations of the underlying limitations. The limitations that apply in each case, with the exception of porosity, are explained in detail in table 2 of the DBV/BDZ data sheet (fig. 7). The restrictions regarding porosity are listed in another table. The following individual criteria are used:

- T1 to T3 designate the texture of the concrete surface and its formation at joints between formwork elements. This is assessed by considering the porosity of the concrete surface and defects caused by loss of cement paste, discrepancies in the surface level and fins at joints between formwork elements.
- P1 to P4 designate the porosity. This is in each case limited by a permissible maximum value for the total area of pores on a test surface measuring 500 x 500 mm (0.25 m²) and covers pore diameters from 2 to 15 mm. Determin-

ing the total pore area manually is a time-consuming, tedious process with only limited accuracy. Computer-assisted photometric methods for determining the porosity will be available soon and will deliver sufficiently accurate results for a reasonable effort. As the porosity when using absorbent formwork panels is of course lower than when using non-absorbent formwork panels, fair-face concrete classes SB 2, SB 3 and SB 4 are allocated different porosity requirements according to the type of formwork panel (s = absorbent, ns = non-absorbent, see fig. 5).

- FT1 to FT3 designate the consistency of the colour of the concrete. The gradations of the individual steps are explained in table 2 (fig. 7). Deviations in colour of any kind caused for any reason are the determining criteria. As absorbent formwork panels generally deliver much better results with regard to consistency of colouring, table 1 specifies FT2 for class SB 4 when using a non-absorbent formwork panel, but FT3 when using an absorbent formwork panel.
- The flatness of a fair-face concrete surface depends primarily on the stiffness of the formwork. If the formwork distorts

as the pressure of the wet concrete increases, this deformation is transferred to the surface of the hardened concrete and can lead to visible deviations in the flatness of the surface. E1 to E3 designate the flatness requirements. The individual criteria regarding flatness refer to certain provisions of DIN 18202 "Dimensional tolerances in building construction – buildings". Fig. 7 outlines the limitations for each flatness tolerance level.

- AF1 to AF4 designate the requirements regarding the formation and appearance of the concrete surface in the vicinity of construction and formwork panel joints. As with the joints between formwork elements, this criterion limits offsets in the level of the surface and defects caused by loss of cement paste.

Despite the high demands, the individual criteria and construction rules for fair-face concrete class SB 4 are intentionally flexible. Class SB 4 is hence an "open class" which also permits the formulation of extraordinary surface properties. Simply the specification of class SB 4 signals to all those involved that the appearance of the surface is very important for the archi-

Fair-face concrete classes and their associated requirements (DBV/BDZ data sheet table 1)

Fair-face concrete class		Examples	Requirements for fair-face concrete surfaces [1,2] cast against formwork depending on class							Further details		Cost
			Texture	Porosity [3]		Consistency of colouring [4]		Flatness	Construction and formwork panel joints	Trial panel [5]	Formwork panel class [6]	
				s	ns	s	ns					
Low requirements	SB 1	Concrete surfaces with low architectural requirements, e.g. basement walls or areas with primarily commercial usage	T1	P1	P1	FT1	FT1	E1	AF1	optional	SHK1	low
Normal requirements	SB 2	Concrete surfaces with normal architectural requirements, e.g. staircase towers, retaining walls	T2	P2	P1	FT2	FT2	E1	AF2	recommended	SHK2	mod.
Special requirements	SB 3	Concrete surfaces with high architectural requirements, e.g. building facades	T2	P3	P2	FT2	FT2	E2	AF3	highly advisable	SHK2	high
	SB 4	Concrete surfaces with special architectural significance, prestigious components in buildings	T3	P4	P3	FT3	FT2	E3	AF4	essential	SHK3	very high

[1] In principle, the architectural effect of the exposed surface of a fair-face concrete class can only be assessed properly by way of its *overall effect*, not by means of individual criteria. The design effect of the surface of any particular class of exposed concrete can be assessed properly only in terms of its overall effect and not on the basis of individual criteria. The absence of individual features mentioned in the data sheet table should not imply an obligation to rectify deficiencies if the overall impression created by the constructional element or structure in question is not impaired in terms of its positive design effect.

[2] These requirements/properties are described in more detail in fig. 7 (table 2).

[3] s = absorbent formwork panel; ns = non-absorbent formwork panel.

[4] The overall impression can only be assessed after a longer period (in some circumstances after several weeks). The consistency of colouring should be assessed from a normal viewing distance according to section 7 of the DBV/BDZ data sheet.

[5] Several trial panels should be produced if necessary.

[6] See fig. 9 (formwork panel classes)

tecture. The specification of the work when planning extraordinary surface qualities should be supplemented by appropriate features or described in some other way. Individual criteria that are incompatible with the desired surface quality should in this case be contractually excluded or limited even further. When doing so, make sure that this does not result in senseless or impossible demands regarding the surface properties. Some of the explanations of the individual criteria for class SB 4 already indicate that the designer should provide a separate, detailed description of the individual requirements.

Formwork panel classes

The specification of formwork panel classes in the DBV/BDZ data sheet is also new (table 3 of the data sheet, see fig. 9). The nature and condition of the formwork panel chosen are important factors affecting the quality of the fair-face concrete finish obtainable. Three formwork panel classes (SHK1 to SHK3) were introduced, and explained and defined by means of a series of practical criteria. The explicit allocation of a formwork panel class to a fair-face concrete class (fig. 5) is intended to guarantee that the formwork panel cho-

sen is suitable for producing the surface quality required. The contractor is obliged to check the condition of the formwork panel before every use of the formwork element. The formwork panel class required is deemed to be satisfied when the entire surface of the formwork panel of the formwork element corresponds to the condition criteria for the respective class as given in fig. 9. After specifying the fair-face concrete class, the designer must then check the condition criteria of the associated formwork panel class to establish whether the expected surface properties can be achieved with the criteria listed. If necessary, the condition criteria can be adapted by introducing further contractual requirements.

The highest formwork panel class (SHK3) is allocated solely to fair-face concrete class SB 4. If this fair-face concrete class is to be extended by the design to encompass extraordinary surface properties as well, the condition criteria of formwork panel class SHK3 should essentially be specified in consultation with the designer.

6   Concrete surfaces satisfying very high architectural requirements (SB 4), crematorium, Berlin, 1998; architects: Axel Schultes Architekten

6

Fair-face concrete

Requirements for fair-face concrete surfaces cast against formwork (DBV/BDZ data sheet table 2)

Criterion	Abbreviation	Requirements/properties [2]
Texture, joints between formwork elements	T1	Essentially closed cement paste or grout surface. Loss of cement paste/grout up to approx. 20 mm wide and approx. 10 mm deep perm. at joints between formwork elements. An impression of the formwork element frame is permissible.
	T2	Closed and essentially uniform concrete surface. Loss of cement paste/grout up to approx. 10 mm wide and approx. 5 mm deep perm. at joints between formwork elements. Offset at joints between elements up to approx. 5 mm is permissible. Fins up to approx. 5 mm high are permissible. An impression of the formwork element frame is permissible.
	T3	Smooth, closed and essentially uniform concrete surface. Loss of cement paste/grout up to approx. 3 mm wide is permissible at joints between formwork elements. Fine, technically unavoidable fins up to approx. 3 mm high are permissible. Other requirements (e.g. joints between elements, frame impression) must be specified in detail.
Porosity	P1–P4	See DBV/BDZ data sheet table 4.
Consistency of colouring	FT1	Light/dark discoloration is permissible. Patches of rust and soiling are not permissible.
	FT2	Consistent, large areas of light/dark discoloration are permissible. Different types and pretreatment of formwork panels and raw materials of different types and origins are not permissible.
	FT3	Large areas of discoloration caused by materials of different types and origins, different types and pretreatment of formwork panels, unsuitable curing of the concrete are not permissible. Minor light/dark discoloration (e.g. minor clouding, minor discoloration) is permissible. Patches of rust and soiling, clearly visible concrete lifts and discoloration are not permissible. Selection of special and suitable release agents is required. *Note: Differences in colour and discoloration cannot be entirely excluded even with very careful workmanship.*
Flatness [1]	E1	Flatness requirements to DIN 18202, table 3, line 5.
	E2	Flatness requirements to DIN 18202, table 3, line 6.
	E3	Flatness requirements to DIN 18202, table 3, line 6. Higher flatness requirements must be specially agreed; the work and measures necessary for this must be specified in detail by the client. *Note: Higher flatness requirements, e.g. to DIN 18202, table 3, line 7, cannot be reliably fulfilled technically.*
Construction and formwork panel joints [3]	AF1	Offset of surfaces up to approx. 10 mm between two concrete pours is permissible.
	AF2	Offset of surfaces up to approx. 10 mm between two concrete pours is permissible. Loss of grout onto the previous concrete pour must be removed in good time. Trapezoidal batten or similar is recommended.
	AF3	Offset of surfaces up to approx. 5 mm between two concrete pours is permissible. Loss of grout onto the previous concrete pour must be removed in good time. Trapezoidal batten or similar is recommended.
	AF4	Concreting operations must be planned in detail. Offset of surfaces up to approx. 5 mm between two concrete pours is permissible. Loss of grout onto the previous concrete pour must be removed in good time. Other requirements (e.g. design of construction and formwork panel joints) must be specified in detail.

[1] Flatness requirements do not apply to worked or textured surfaces.
[2] Take into account sections of 5.1.2 and 7 of the DBV/BDZ data sheet.
[3] Construction joints remain visible.

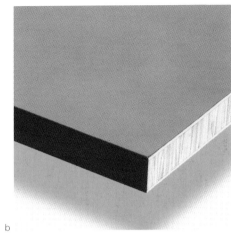

8a   b   c

Design and award of contract

Although the production of exposed concrete surfaces represents a particularly difficult building task, inadequately formulated tenders and building contracts often cause additional, sometimes even the most serious, difficulties when trying to produce fair-face concrete surfaces. Experience has shown that during the tender phase many contractors are very reticent to ask questions regarding the resolution and explanation of ambiguous contractual formulations. In order to win the contract, the tenderer often accepts the status quo even though he has calculated his price based on ambiguous specifications and obvious differences of opinion regarding the target of the contract come to light as soon as the contract is signed.

Ambiguous and incomplete designs and contracts are usually the outcome of ignorance and lack of "gleanable" parameters and advice. It was for this reason that extra attention was given to revising and expanding the design-related content of the DBV/BDZ data sheet. The introduction of fair-face concrete classes reinforces this goal and is intended to simplify the planning of the desired appearance. Besides a complete overview of the formwork and formwork panel systems currently available and the surface finishes they can be expected to produce, the designer is provided with an overview of the minimum specification he must provide. There is also a checklist for checking the design documents for coherency and completeness (fig. 11).

When applying the regulations of the DBV/BDZ data sheet, the designer must ensure that all design and construction details are already available in the tender documents and are recognisable as

8 Various boards for formwork panels:
   a veneer plywood with film coating, mildly absorbent
   b timber–synthetic material composite with core of timber battens and facings of fleece-reinforced film coating
   c highly compressed wood-based board, ground finish, mildly absorbent

Formwork panel classes (DBV/BDZ data sheet table 3)

	SHK 1	SHK 2	SHK 3 [2]
Drilled holes	Close off with plastic caps	Permissible in the form of repairs [1]	Not permissible
Nail and screw holes	Permissible	Permissible if no chips or splinters	Permissible in the form of repairs [1] if agreed with the client
Damage to formwork panel caused by poker vibrator	Permissible	Not permissible [3]	Not permissible
Scratches	Permissible	Permissible in the form of repairs [1]	Permissible in the form [1] of repairs [1] if agreed with the client
Concrete residue	Permissible in depressions (nail holes, craters, etc.), no residue adhering over large areas	Not permissible	Not permissible
Cement streaks	Permissible	Permissible	Permissible if agreed with the client
Swelling of the formwork panel in the vicinity of screws and nails ("rippling")	Permissible	Not permissible [3]	Not permissible
Repairs1 [1]	Permissible	Permissible	Permissible if agreed with the client

[1] Check repairs to the formwork panel. Repairs to formwork panel should be carried out by qualified persons in a professional and workmanlike manner. The elements should be inspected before each application to ensure that they comply with the specified condition.
[2] Practical experience has shown that multiple uses of the formwork panel can thus be ruled out.
9 [3] May be permitted if agreed with the client.

such, and do not first appear later in the building contract. The work described in the tender documents and the building contract must match exactly, unless modified details are negotiated when the contract is awarded.

The specification should include the actual items in the bill of quantities plus any contractual performance conditions, insofar as they cause costs and work. These include, above all, the contractual measures regarding quality control and site management explained elsewhere in this book (see pp. 66–69), which are also ideal for the management of building operations involving fair-face concrete surfaces. Such measures and requirements have an affect on the costs and must be included in the tender documents.

As the architectural ideas regarding the appearance of surfaces are often difficult to convey in the specification, the tender documents should be handed over at a preliminary meeting. It is advisable here to restrict the number of tenderers to a manageable group. The meeting offers a number of advantages which the designer should exploit, particularly if he is also responsible for the site management at a later date:
- The detailed information and explanations discussed in the meeting with the tenderer should be recorded in writing in order to safeguard the designer in the case of later disputes.
- If the designer feels it is helpful or necessary, he can make references to surfaces on existing buildings in order to illustrate the outcome required and make it compulsory for the tenderer to undertake a supervised visit to the site.
- The designer can obtain a personal impression of the abilities and commitment of the tenderer. He can check and inquire about references provided by the tenderer. The particular difficulties and important aspects of the works and the procedures envisaged by the tenderer can be discussed in advance.
In reality, fair-face concrete is, in the end, always the result of the attempt to create surfaces with a certain appearance using the means laid down in the contract and the materials available on the building site under the prevailing conditions (season, weather, etc.). As it is in most cases difficult to achieve an exact match between the quality achieved and the ideas of the architect, it is also helpful for the designer to compare his ideas with the feasibility of the building site in practical trials, and to

specify the surface characteristics in the contract based on knowledge of the practical options.

This approach is demonstrated below using the example of smooth fair-face concrete surfaces. In doing so, the allocation of responsibilities to designer or contractor are always upheld despite the need for the designer to become fully involved in the issues of everyday building operations (target–path separation, see pp. 58–72).

Situation

The architect proposes smooth fair-face concrete for the wall surfaces in all public areas as well as the classrooms and offices of a school building. His idea regarding the appearance of the fair-face concrete surfaces is based on surface features that were achieved on another building. He has photographs of those finished surfaces.

General approach

As the appearance of the fair-face concrete surfaces is difficult to describe in the contract, the final properties of the surfaces are to be decided after trials on the building site under the local conditions. In preparing the tender and contract, practical tests using trial panels shall be specified in order to achieve the desired result.

Tender
The final, contractually agreed properties of the fair-face concrete surfaces are to be specified by means of trial panels. Nevertheless, it must be possible for the tenderer to assess and calculate the price of the work required to produce the desired quality. The designer decides on the following procedure:

· In the contract the fair-face concrete surfaces are assigned to fair-face concrete class SB 3 according to table 1 of the DBV/BDZ data sheet.
· The bill of quantities includes an item for producing three trial panels with component-like dimensions (including foundation, protection, maintenance, dismantling and disposal).
· The tender is supplemented by "additional technical conditions of contract" in preparation for the later contractual configuration. Components requiring fair-face concrete are identified in the bill of quantities by adding the following note: "The additional technical conditions of contract shall apply regarding the appearance of the surfaces."
· A formwork layout drawing is produced to assist the pricing work. If this is to be available with all details for every component during the later construction phase, the architect can delegate the production of an accurate formwork layout to the contractor in the contract. In this case the tender must include typical details to enable the tenderer to identify the cost of the production of formwork layout drawings and the difficulty (costs) of constructing the formwork.
· The surface characteristics of the fair-face concrete are specified in the additional technical conditions of contract thus: "The following requirements shall apply to fair-face concrete works: The features and regulations of fair-face concrete class SB 3 according to table 1 of the DBV/BDZ data sheet, 2004 edition, shall apply to the appearance of the exposed surfaces and their construction. The exposed surfaces shall be constructed smooth using non-absorbent formwork panels and in accordance with the instructions of the formwork layout drawing. The selection of the formwork panels and concrete mixes used for producing the trial panels shall be carried out in consultation with the architect. Contractual reference panels for accepting the works shall be chosen from the trial panels. The surface features of the reference panels

shall govern the acceptance of the contractually agreed fair-face concrete surfaces."
· "Special conditions of contract" are included in the tender in which the designer formulates the performance conditions with respect to quality control and site management applicable to this project (see p. 71).
· In the case of selective tendering, the tender documents are handed over in a meeting. During the meeting the architect can use the texts of the tender to explain the desired appearance of the fair-face concrete surfaces to the tenderer and perhaps present photographs and any other supplementary information (eventually coupled with a visit to an existing building). The technical procedures required to produce the trial panels and the contractual provisions regarding quality control and site management in the special conditions of contract can be explained and discussed. The important points of the meeting should be recorded in writing. These measures are intended to provide sufficient information to enable the tenderer to estimate and price the works. At this stage neither the architect nor the contractor knows the final contractual surface properties. However, as these are to be selected from trial panels, they can be achieved with all likelihood using the technical means allowed for in the price.

Building contract
The specifications in the tender, the additional technical conditions of contract and the special conditions of contract are absorbed into the building contract without any modifications.

Site management
The architect and technical representatives of the successful contractor meet with potential formwork panel manufacturers immediately after award of contract. The materials for producing the trial panels are also specified at this time. Similar meetings are arranged with the potential ready-mixed concrete suppliers. Unless the contract states otherwise, the contractor has the right to propose all the materials.

10 Grid ceiling in fair-face concrete, building for members of the German parliament, Paul Löbe House, Berlin, 2001; architects: Stefan Braunfels Architekten

---

"Checklist" of architectural features

· Fair-face concrete class according to fig. 5
· Formwork and formwork panel system
· Surface texture (choice of formwork panel or subsequent surface treatment)
· Formation of joints between formwork elements
· Formwork ties and tie holes (position, formation and making good)
· Subdivision of the surface (dimensions of formwork elements, formwork textures, pattern of joints, arrangement of formwork tie holes, etc.)
· Joints (position, direction, width and details)
· Detailing of corners and edges (e.g. keen, chamfered)
· Colouring (selected cements, aggregates, pigments, glazes, paints)
· Surface finish of areas not cast against formwork (e.g. top surfaces of spandrel panels)

12a

A "fair-face concrete team" is set up in advance of the work. This team includes at least one person with technical responsibility from the design team, the contractor and the ready-mixed concrete supplier, and in some cases the formwork supplier as well. The fair-face concrete team should meet regularly. The first meeting serves to specify the procedure for producing the trial panels, which are produced in stages, the joint assessment of the outcome of one trial panel determining the next step. At the same time as producing the trial panels, technical variations of the method can be tested on secondary contractual building components without fair-face concrete stipulations (basement, plant rooms, etc.).
In order to specify the properties of the contractually agreed fair-face concrete surfaces, the architect selects one or two suitable trial panels and labels these. The formal specification of these surfaces as contractually agreed references is achieved by adding a supplementary agreement between client and contractor to the existing contract.

Workmanship requirements – defining responsibilities
The explanations regarding the production of fair-face concrete surfaces given in chapter 6 of the DBV/BDZ data sheet are supplemented by appendices A–D. These contain detailed information for the production of the surface features required by the contract. The current edition of the data sheet supports and binds the contractor by way of far more comprehensive and detailed regulations (compared to earlier editions). Owing to developments in concrete technology, the DBV/BDZ data sheet does not include any binding information regarding concrete mix and consistence because more recent findings have shown that it is no longer advisable to place restrictions on such criteria. In the light of technological changes brought about by the latest plasticisers, only recommendations are given.

With a view to providing a sound contractual division of responsibilities, it is the duty and freedom of the contractor to choose the concrete mix required – from the multitude of options – for the successful realisation of the fair-face concrete quality specified in the contract. Building contracts for the production of fair-face concrete frequently contain provisions relating to concrete mixes or methods of placement. Such provisions are, however, for the most part technically erroneous and prevent the contractor from carrying out his work in a proper practical manner.

Assessment
The introduction of fair-face concrete classes, which are principally defined by way of individual criteria, means it is now natural to question whether these individual criteria are fulfilled when assessing the work. However, concentrating on assessing the individual criteria is not really the aim of the data sheet and does not correspond to the usual approach of the architect when assessing a fair-face concrete surface. Concentrating exclusively on individual criteria for an assessment can lead to the rejection of fair-face concrete surfaces because certain individual criteria do not meet the standard even though the overall impression satisfies the architect. It is therefore not advisable to define the overall impression of an exposed surface by means of the sum of the compliance of individual criteria. For the designer, it is solely the overall impression of a surface that forms the key assessment criterion and is the only way of comparing the work with his own ideas. In the end, this is the only sensible way of assessing a surface.

If the overall impression corresponds to the designer's ideas, the work is accepted and the individual criteria are not assessed. The individual criteria for the applicable fair-face concrete class are used for the further assessment only when the overall impression of a surface does not correspond to the contractually agreed ideas of the designer. In this case it is the job of designer and contractor to analyse the deviations by means of the individual criteria assessment in order to prevent the same problems happening again in the project. Even a graded assessment of deviations and their translation into contractual consequences can be carried out simply and understandably via the assessment of individual criteria.

The viewing distance and the age of the surface being assessed are important factors in the assessment of an overall impression. It is not possible to stipulate the "right" age for assessing a fair-face concrete surface. In the case of deviations regarding consistency of colouring, light–dark patches and similar phenomena on fresh concrete, the assessment of the surface should initially be postponed to a later date. In such situations make sure that the surface is as dry as possible by the time of the final assessment. Some deviations take years to become less obtrusive or even disappear completely (figs 12a and b). However, it is impossible to predict their changes over a longer period of time. On the other hand, pores, bleeding and flatness problems will not improve with age.

In addition to choosing the right time for assessing a fair-face concrete surface or structure, the viewing distance can also influence the outcome. The unprejudiced observer of a surface with typical dimensions will tend to stand about 1-3 m away when asked to assess a fair-face con-

crete surface on a building. This distance is a good compromise which enables both details and the overall surface to be perceived well in average lighting conditions. However, the viewing distance for assessing the overall impression in the sense of the architect's ideas is based on other criteria. We must distinguish here between observing the structure and observing the individual component. An appropriate distance for assessing the structure is the distance from which the main parts of the structure can be perceived. In other words, it varies depending on the place from where the building is observed.

Individual components should be assessed from the distance at which the later users of the building will normally perceive those components. This rule of thumb can lead to different opinions on the correct viewing distance, particularly in the case of surfaces adjacent to expansive public areas (e.g. halls, squares). In such cases the assessment should be carried out from various distances.

12 "Improvement with time", Saggio, Ferrari dealer, Würzburg, 2001; architect: Thomas Mensing
 a patchy discoloration on the concrete surfaces after striking the formwork
 b the improvement after about eight months

12 b

Appendices

Standards and directives (selection)

Concrete

DIN EN 206-1
Concrete – Part 1: Specification, performance, production and conformity (compiled according to DIN special report 100 "Beton")

DIN EN 206-1
Concrete – Part 1: Specification, performance, production and conformity (compiled according to DIN special report 100 "Beton")

DIN 1045-1
Concrete, reinforced and prestressed concrete structures – Part 1: Design and construction

DAfStb booklet 525
Explanatory texts to DIN 1045-1 (German only)

DIN 1045-2
Concrete, reinforced and prestressed concrete structures – Part 2: Concrete; Specification, properties, production and conformity; Application rules for DIN EN 206-1 (compiled according to DIN special report 100 "Beton")

DIN special report 100 "Beton"
Compilation of DIN EN 206-1 and DIN 1045-2

DIN 1045-3
Concrete, reinforced and prestressed concrete structures – Part 3: Execution of structures

DIN 1045-4
Concrete, reinforced and prestressed concrete structures – Part 4: Additional rules for the production and conformity control of prefabricated elements

DAfStb booklet 526
Explanatory texts to DIN EN 206-1, DIN 1045-2, DIN 1045-3, DIN 1045-4 and DIN 4226

DIN 4030
Assessment of water, soil and gases for their aggressiveness to concrete

DIN 4102-4
Fire behaviour of building materials and building components – Part 4: Synopsis and application of classified building materials, components and special components

DIN V 4108-4
Thermal insulation and energy economy in buildings – Part 4: characteristic values relating to thermal insulation and protection against moisture

DIN 4235
Compacting of concrete by vibrating

DIN 18202
Dimensional tolerances in building construction – buildings

DIN 18218
Pressure of fresh concrete on vertical formwork

DIN EN 13369
Common rules for precast concrete products

DIN 18203-1
Tolerances in building construction – Part 1: Prefabricated components made of concrete, reinforced concrete and prestressed concrete

DAfStb guidelines (German only):
Betonbau beim Umgang mit wassergefährdenden Stoffen
Beton mit rezykliertem Zuschlag
Selbstverdichtender Beton
Vorbeugende Massnahmen gegen schädigende Alkalireaktionen im Beton
Wasserundurchlässige Bauwerke aus Beton

Concrete additives/admixtures

DIN EN 934-2
Admixtures for concrete, mortar and grout – Part 2: Concrete admixtures

DIN V 20000-100 (pre-standard)
Application of building products in structures – Part 100: Concrete admixtures according to DIN EN 934-2

DAfStb guideline: Verwendung von Flugasche nach DIN EN 450 im Betonbau

DIN EN 12878
Pigments for colouring of building materials based on cement and/or lime – Specifications and methods of test

DIN 51043
Trass; requirements, tests

Reinforcement

DIN 488
Reinforcing steels; grades, properties, marking

DIN EN 10080
Steel for the reinforcement of concrete – Weldable reinforcing steel – General, see DIN 488

Aggregate

DIN 4226-2
Aggregates for concrete – Part 2: Aggregates of porous structure (lightweight aggregates)

DIN 4226-100
Aggregates for concrete and mortar – Part 100: Recycled aggregates

DIN EN 12620
Aggregates for concrete

DIN EN 13055-1
Lightweight aggregates – Part 1: Lightweight aggregates for concrete, mortar and grout

DIN V 20000-103 (pre-standard)
Use of building products in construction works – Part 103: Aggregates according to DIN EN 12620

DIN V 20000-104 (pre-standard)
Use of building products in construction works – Part 104: Lightweight aggregates according to DIN EN 13055-1

Cement

DIN EN 197-1
Cement – Part 1: Composition, specifications and conformity criteria for common cements

DIN 1164
Special cement

Mixing water

DIN EN 1008
Mixing water for concrete – Specification for sampling, testing and assessing the suitability of water, including water recovered from processes in the concrete industry, as mixing water for concrete

Bibliography (selection)

Cement data sheets (German only) published by the Bundesverband der Deutschen Zementindustrie e.V. (can be downloaded free of charge from www.bdzement.de or www.beton.org):

Concrete technology

B1, Zemente und ihre Herstellung, 10/2005

B2, Gesteinskörnungen für Normalbeton, 10/2004

B3, Betonzusätze, Zusatzmittel und Zusatzstoffe, 09/2005

B4, Frischbeton – Eigenschaften und Prüfungen, 12/2002

B5, Überwachung von Beton auf Baustellen, 12/2004

B6, Transportbeton, 08/2002

B7, Bereiten und Verarbeiten von Beton, 08/2002

B8, Nachbehandlung von Beton, 11/2002

B9, Expositionsklassen von Beton und besondere Betoneigenschaften, 12/2004

B10, Schwerbeton /Strahlenschutzbeton, 01/2002

B11, Massenbeton, 12/2000

B12, Unterwasserbeton, 01/1999

B13, Leichtbeton, 09/1998

B16, Hochfester Beton / Hochleistungsbeton, 10/2002

B18, Risse im Beton, 02/2003

B22, Arbeitsfugen, 01/2002

B24, Betonstahl und Verlegen der Bewehrung, 09/1998

B26, Füllen von Rissen, 06/2003

B27, Ausblühung – Entstehung, Vermeidung, Beseitigung, 12/2003

Buildings and structures

H1, Baulicher Brandschutz mit Beton, 06/2000

H2, Begrünte Dächer, 10/1998

H3, Flachdächer aus Beton, 01/1999

H4, Wärmedämmputz, 08/1999

H5, Keller – richtig gebaut, 09/1998

H6, Schallschutz mit Beton im Wohnungsbau, 01/2002

H8, Sichtbeton – Gestaltung von Betonoberflächen, 08/1999

H9, Schalung für Beton, 08/1999

H10, Wasserundurchlässige Betonbauwerke, 10/2005

H11, Sichtmauerwerk aus Beton (Normalbeton), 10/1998

H12, Energieeffizientes Bauen mit Beton – Vereinfachtes Verfahren nach EnEV, 03/2003

Data sheets (German only) of the Deutscher Beton- & Bautechnik-Verein:

Abstandhalter, July 2002

Betondeckung und Bewehrung – Sicherung der Betondeckung beim Entwerfen, Herstellen und Einbauen der Bewehrung sowie des Betons, July 2002

Betonierbarkeit von Bauteilen aus Beton und Stahlbeton – Planungs- und Ausführungsempfehlungen für den Betoneinbau, November 1996

Betonieren im Winter, August 1999
Betonoberfläche – Betonrandzone, November 1996

Betonschalungen, May 1999

Nicht geschalte Betonoberfläche, August 1996

Selbstverdichtender Beton, December 2004

Trennmittel für Beton – Teil A: Hinweise zur Auswahl und Anwendung, March 1997

Deutscher Beton- & Bautechnik-Verein e.V., Bundesverband der Deutschen Zementindustrie e.V. (pub.): Merkblatt Sichtbeton. Berlin/Düsseldorf, 2004

Books

Bennett, David: The Art of Precast Concrete. Basel, 2005

Bertrams-Vosskamp, Ulrike et al.: Betonwerkstein-Handbuch. Düsseldorf, 2001

Bauberatung Zement (pub.): Bauteilkatalog. Düsseldorf, 2005

Bose, Thomas; Pickhardt, Roland: Beton – Herstellung nach Norm. Düsseldorf, 2005

Cemsuisse, Institute for the History and Theory of Architecture at the Swiss Federal Institute of Technology, Zürich (pub.): Architekturpreis Beton 05. Zürich, 2005

Döhring, Wolfgang et al.: Fassaden mit Betonfertigteilen. Düsseldorf, 2000

Eifert, Helmut; Bethge, Wolfgang: Beton – Prüfung nach Norm. Düsseldorf, 2005

Fehlhaber, Jörg M.: Metapher Beton oder die Rettung der Architektur. Düsseldorf, 1995

Hassler, Uta; Schmidt, Hartwig (ed.): Häuser aus Beton. Tübingen, 2004

Heene, Gerd: Baustelle Pantheon. Düsseldorf, 2004
Hegger, Manfred et al.: Construction Materials Manual. Munich/Basel, 2005

Kapellmann, Klaus D.; Langen, Werner: Einführung in die VOB/B. Munich, 2003

Kind-Barkauskas, Friedbert (pub.): Beton und Farbe. Munich, 2003

Kind-Barkauskas et al.: Concrete Construction Manual. Munich/Basel, 2002

Lamprecht, Heinz Otto.: Opus Caementitium. Düsseldorf, 1996

Lindner, Gerhard; Schmitz-Riol, Erik: Systembauweise im Wohnungsbau. Düsseldorf, 2001

Lohmeyer, Gottfried; Ebeling, Karsten: Weisse Wannen einfach und sicher. Düsseldorf, 2004

Middel, Matthias et al.: Bauphysik nach Mass. Düsseldorf, 2003

Müller, Petra: Beton in der Architektur. Düsseldorf, 2001

Neunast, Armin; Lange, Friederike: Leichtbeton Handbuch. Düsseldorf, 2001

Pfeifer, Günter; Liebers, Antje: Sichtbeton. Düsseldorf, 2005

Primus, Illo-Frank: Massivabsorber. Düsseldorf, 1995

Rüegg, Arthur et al.: Die Unschuld des Betons. Zürich, 2004

Schwerm, Dieter: Ausbaudetails im Fertigteilbau. Düsseldorf, 2002

Verein Deutscher Zementwerke (pub.): Zement-Taschenbuch 2002. Düsseldorf, 2002

Weber, Robert; Tegelaar Rudolf: Guter Beton. Düsseldorf, 2005

Wieland, Dieter: Gebaute Lebensräume. Düsseldorf, 1987

Willems, Wolfgang et al.: Wärmebrücken- und Konstruktionsatlas. Düsseldorf, 2005

Zeitler, Ralf: Bemessung im Stahlbetonbau nach DIN 1045-1. Düsseldorf, 2005

Trade journals

Baumeister, Beton, 07/2005

Beton 03/2005

Beton-Information Spezial, 04/2005: Sichtbeton – Planung und Ausführung

DBZ, Beton, 06/2004

Detail, Bauen mit Beton, 01/2001

Detail, Bauen mit Beton, 04/2003

Detail, Bauen mit Beton, 01 & 02/2006

Werk, Bauen + Wohnen, Beton, 01 & 02/2005

Zeitschrift für Architektur (international examples of contemporary use of concrete), 05/2004

Index

Appendices

Picture credits

Photographs not specifically credited were taken by the authors, provided by the manufacturer or supplied from the DETAIL archives.

page 6:
Christian Richters, Münster

page 8:
Richard Bryant/arcaid

pages 9 left, 89 (fig. 6):
Verlag Bau + Technik, Düsseldorf

page 9 right:
Sigrid Neubert, Munich

pages 12, 13:
Studio Ernst/Kieswerke Rheinbach

pages 14 top, 17, 24, 89 (figs 3, 4, 5, 7):
Bundesverband der Deutschen Zement-industrie, Berlin

page 14 bottom:
Institute for Building Materials, University of the German Armed Forces, Munich

page 15:
from: René Walther: Bauen mit Beton, Berlin 1997; photo: A. Herzog

page 22 left:
from: Iken, Lackner, Zimmer, Wöhnl: Handbuch der Betonprüfung. Düsseldorf, 2003

pages 23, 58:
Beton Marketing Nord, Sehnde

pages 26, 27:
Shinkenchiku-sha, Tokyo

pages 28, 30, 31:
LiTraCon GmbH, Aachen/Csongrád

page 29 left:
Verrazzo

page 29 right:
Wausau Tile, Wausau/Wisconsin

page 32:
Institute for Textile Engineering, RWTH Aachen

pages 33–37:
Chair of Construction 2, RWTH Aachen

page 38:
IEZ Natterer GmbH, Saulburg/Wiesenfelden

pages 40–42:
Roland Krippner, Munich

page 43:
G. Feldmann, Munich

page 44:
Sebastian Greuner, Berlin

pages 48, 68–70, 75 bottom, 80 centre, 85 top, 85 bottom left:
Frank Kaltenbach, Munich

pages 52, 53 bottom, 54, 55 bottom, 56, 57, 82, 83 right, 84, 85 bottom right, 86 top, 87 bottom left, 87 centre, 87 bottom right:
Michael Heinrich, Munich

page 60:
Peri, Weissenhorn

pages 62, 99:
Westag & Getalit AG, Rheda-Wiedenbrück

pages 66, 67:
Züblin Wolff & Müller, Stuttgart

page 71:
Martin Schuppenhauer, Berlin

page 72:
Ruedi Walti, Basel

page 73 top:
Klaus Schädler AG, Triesenberg

page 73 bottom:
Thomas Flechtner, La Sagne

page 74:
Jan Bitter, Berlin

page 75 top:
ABT Adviseurs in Bouwtechniek, Arnhem/Delft

pages 76, 77:
Serge Demailly, F–Saint Cyr sur Mer

page 78:
César San Millán, ES–Madrid

page 80 right:
from: Francesco dal Co, Tadao Ando: Complete Works. London, 2000

page 81 top left:
Klemens Ortmeyer, Braunschweig

page 81 top right & bottom:
Andreas Meck, Munich

page 83 left, 87 top:
Susanne Frank, Munich

page 86 bottom:
Werner Schad, Munich

page 88:
Christoph Kreutzenbeck, Wuppertal

page 89 (figs 8a–f):
Dyckerhoff Weiss AG, Wiesbaden

pages 91, 97:
Werner Huthmacher, Berlin

page 94:
Röschert + Schäfer, Architekten + Ingenieure, Volkach

page 95:
Philippe Ruault, Nantes

page 101:
Hannes Fiala, Kriftel

pages 102, 103:
Thomas Mensing, Würzburg

page 104:
Timothy Hursley, Little Rock, Arkansas

Full-page plates

page 6:
Football stadium, Braga
Souto Moura Arquitectos, Porto

page 44:
Former "Ahornblatt" restaurant, Berlin
Ulrich Müther

page 48:
House C, Park Village, Munich
Lauber Architekten, Munich

page 78:
Faculty building, Pamplona
Ignacio Vicens & José Antonio Ramos, Madrid

page 104:
Church, Louisiana
Trahan Architects, Baton Rouge

Cover photographs

top:
Swimming pool, Arzúa
Antonio Raya, Carlos Quintáns, Cristóbal Crespo, La Coruña
photo: Christoph Kreutzenbeck, Wuppertal

centre:
Conference pavilion, Weil am Rhein
Tadao Ando, Osaka
photo: Andreas Meck, Munich